Wallace-Stauffer Debate

Held Sunday, March 7, 1937 Wichita, Kansas

PROPOSITIONS

Infant Baptism

The Lord's Supper

Stenographically Reported by Miss Crystal Norfleet
Edited (2014) by Bradley S. Cobb
ISBN: 979-8-3303-1095-1
Original Copyright BY GERVIAS KNOX (G.K.) WALLACE 1937

Reprinted by Cobb Publishing, 2024

Other books available from

COBB PUBLISHING

Alexander Campbell: A Collection (Volume 1)

Abner Jones: A Collection (Volume 1)

Sketches of Our Pioneers:
a Brief Restoration Movement History

The Prodigal Slave:
a Study of the Letter to Philemon

Fight for the Faith:
a Study of the Letter from Jude

The Beatitudes: A Sermon Collection

Toils and Struggles of the Olden Times:
The Autobiography of Elder Samuel Rogers

Sermons on First Corinthians
by George W. DeHoff

The Oliphant-Smith Debate

Pardee Butler: The Definitive Collection

The Wallace/Stauffer Debate is published by Cobb Publishing, Charleston, Arkansas 2024.

Table of Contents

Introduction

The following discussion was held Sunday afternoon, March 7, 1937, in Wichita, Kansas, between two Wichita preachers: Dr. E.E. Stauffer, pastor of the St. Paul's Lutheran Church and G. K. Wallace, minister of the church of Christ, University and Walnut.

Dr. Stauffer is the president of the Wichita Ministerial Association of Wichita, and has been pastor of the St. Paul's Lutheran Church for fifteen years.

Mr. Wallace has been the minister of the University and Walnut Church of Christ for nearly eight years.

Each minister had the privilege of asking questions and these questions were to be answered immediately.

This discussion was brought about by an invitation being extended to Mr. Wallace to meet Dr. Stauffer and discuss, in the presence of some members of the Lutheran Church and some members of the church of Christ, some questions over which they differed. Mr. Wallace insisted on having a public discussion but Dr. Stauffer declined. So it was arranged to have the "conference," as Dr. Stauffer preferred to call it, at his study, located in the St. Paul's Lutheran Church building. Only the elect were allowed to attend.

After a prayer, led by Dr. Stauffer, the following conversation introduced the discussion:

Dr. Stauffer: When Mrs. Maack spoke to me and asked about this, the other day, and said she would like to meet here, I said that I would be very glad to come, and each of us tell what we believe, but I wouldn't enter into any arguments. That isn't the purpose. That isn't my purpose at any rate, although I shall be glad to answer any questions.

Mr. Wallace: As I understand, there were two questions—infant baptism and the Lord's Supper, which they were particularly interested in. If it is agreeable, you present your views on infant baptism, then I will present what I believe the Bible teaches about it. Then you present your teaching on the Lord's Supper and I shall then present what I believe the Bible teaches about it. If you care to make any rebuttal, it is all right.

DR. STAUFFER'S FIRST SPEECH

Dr. Stauffer: My purpose is to state what we believe the Bible teaches concerning those questions. First, I want to ask you: Do you believe in the Scriptures? In God, the Father?

Mr. Wallace: Yes, sir.

Dr. Stauffer: And you believe in Jesus Christ, His Son?

Mr. Wallace: Yes, sir.

Dr. Stauffer: Conceived of the Holy Spirit?

Mr. Wallace: Yes, sir.

Dr. Stauffer: Born of the virgin, Mary?

Mr. Wallace: Yes, sir

Dr. Stauffer: That He suffered?

Mr. Wallace: Yes, sir.

Dr. Stauffer: And was crucified?

Mr. Wallace: Yes, sir.

Dr. Stauffer: And that He was dead and buried?

Mr. Wallace: Yes, sir.

Dr. Stauffer: And that He rose again?

Mr. Wallace: Yes, sir.

Dr. Stauffer: And you believe in God the Holy Ghost?

Mr. Wallace: I believe in God and the Holy Ghost.

Dr. Stauffer: And you believe in the Christian church?

Mr. Wallace: I believe in the church of Christ. I do not use the word "Christian" as an adjective, when applied to the church.

Dr. Stauffer: You realize the Bible teaches us they were first called Christians at Antioch? I believe in what we mean by the "Christian Church."

Mr. Wallace: I believe in the Church of the New Testament.

Dr. Stauffer: You believe in the communion of the Saints?

Mr. Wallace: Yes, sir.

Dr. Stauffer: And you believe in the forgiveness of sin?

Mr. Wallace: Yes, sir.

Dr. Stauffer: And you believe in the resurrection of the body?

Mr. Wallace: Yes, sir.

Dr. Stauffer: You believe in everlasting life?

Mr. Wallace: Yes, sir.

Dr. Stauffer: You believe Christ will come again to judge the living and the dead?

Mr. Wallace: I do.

Dr. Stauffer: Well, we believe all of that, so there is at least a place where we do not disagree. And you believe, I suppose, that all those things which I called attention to are taught in the Bible?

Mr. Wallace: Yes, sir.

Dr. Stauffer: And the fatherhood of God? The saviorhood of Jesus?

Mr. Wallace: I am not sure that I understand your meaning —"fatherhood of God."

Dr. Stauffer: God, the Father, created all things.

Mr. Wallace: I believe God created all things.

Dr. Stauffer: And Jesus Christ is the Savior?

Mr. Wallace: Yes, sir.

Dr. Stauffer: And that when Jesus Christ ascended to the right hand of God, the Father, He promised to send a Comforter, the Holy Ghost?

Mr. Wallace: Yes, sir.

Dr. Stauffer: And that he did take the things of grace and confirm them unto us?

Mr. Wallace: Yes, sir.

Dr. Stauffer: We believe all that. We believe that God had a church, the church of the Old Testament, and that it was just as much His church as the one in the New. Don't you believe that through that church and faith in Christ, the Messiah who was to come, they were saved?

Mr. Wallace: Yes.

Dr. Stauffer: By faith in Christ who was to come?

Mr. Wallace: Yes.

Dr. Stauffer: Through the covenant?

Mr. Wallace: Through the covenant under which they lived.

Dr. Stauffer: And it was just as divine as the covenant under which we live.

Mr. Wallace: That is true.

Dr. Stauffer: And that church was just as much God's church as the church we have today?

Mr. Wallace: Yes, but they were not the same institution.

Dr. Stauffer: Not the same institution?

Mr. Wallace: That is right.

Dr. Stauffer: Well, of course, that depends upon what you mean. Could we have had the church which we have on earth today, the church of Christ, the church which He instituted, the church which He established—could we have had it if it hadn't been for the Old Testament church?

Mr. Wallace: We could not.

Dr. Stauffer: So the New Testament Church is the outgrowth of God's divine manifestations through the prophets until the fullness of time had come in which the Savior of Man appeared on earth?

Mr. Wallace: The Old Testament law was fulfilled—it was a schoolmaster to bring us to Christ.

Dr. Stauffer: To bring us to Christ, creator of all the universe and all plans of salvation, before His appearing on earth or after. Is that right?

Mr. Wallace: I think so.

Dr. Stauffer: And all things were made by Him, and without Him was not anything made that was made?

Mr. Wallace: That is true.

Dr. Stauffer: All right. Now, you want me to tell you what we believe about baptism.

Mr. Wallace: Yes, sir.

Dr. Stauffer: In the first place, I suppose you are acquainted with the fact that all through the centuries, even as far back as St. Augustine, who wrote seven volumes on the subject of baptism, there have been differences of opinion concerning baptism. You are aware of it, of course?

Mr. Wallace: Yes, sir.

Dr. Stauffer: And you are not unmindful of the fact that all through the centuries there were differences of opinion by men who were Christian men?

Mr. Wallace: Yes, sir.

Dr. Stauffer: And that they were Christians, as others who have gone after?

Mr. Wallace: I couldn't say.

Dr. Stauffer: You wouldn't?

Mr. Wallace: I don't know whether they were Christians or not.

Dr. Stauffer: How do you judge? May I ask you, how do you arrive at whether a person is a Christian or not?

Mr. Wallace: By what the Bible teaches.

Dr. Stauffer: All right. Then, if you have a person come into your denomination, do you judge whether they are Christian or not?

Mr. Wallace: No, sir.

Dr. Stauffer: Then you would say you don't know whether they are Christians?

Mr. Wallace: I only know that if they obey the gospel, they are Christians.

Dr. Stauffer: You believe in the supreme authority of Christ?

Mr. Wallace: I do.

Dr. Stauffer: The Bible the only infallible rule of faith and practice?

Mr. Wallace: Yes, sir.

Dr. Stauffer: That salvation is by faith alone, and not by works?

Mr. Wallace: No, sir. We believe it is *not* by faith alone.

Dr. Stauffer: Not by faith alone? What do you think of Paul's statement in Ephesians where he says we are saved not by works lest any man should boast?

Mr. Wallace: Please state where Paul said you are justified by *faith only*.

Dr. Stauffer: In Romans (5:1), I believe, you are justified by faith.

Mr. Wallace: Does he say "faith *only*"?

Dr. Stauffer: By faith alone and not by works.

Mr. Wallace: Why do you say that?

Dr. Stauffer: Because he says in Ephesians we are not saved by works—it is by faith, not our works.

Mr. Wallace: You mean, Doctor, when Paul said not by works, he meant not by obedience?

Dr. Stauffer: If you make it not by obedience, no. It is not by our obedience; it is by Christ's obedience.

Mr. Wallace: You mean a man can be saved without obeying Christ?

Dr. Stauffer: There is nothing we do towards Christ's salvation—our salvation. He purchased our salvation by His death on the cross, and there is nothing that you or I can add to the sacrifice of Christ to make our salvation. Our salvation has been purchased by His death, and there is nothing I can do except accept the salvation which He has offered. I can't do a thing and no man on earth has ever done anything towards his salvation. Christ alone died upon the cross—He has wrought our full salvation and I can't do a thing—and neither can you. You can't even, nor I can't even, accept or have faith without the Holy Spirit operating to enlighten us so that we may know about Christ, and the Holy Spirit through the Word begets faith in our hearts so that we even have the ability to have faith in our God. It is not of ourselves, it is the Word of God.

Mr. Wallace: (interrupting): Tell us where the Holy Spirit puts faith in our hearts.

Dr. Stauffer: Through His Word. "How shall they hear without a preacher?" You never knew anyone to become a Christian apart from the Word. It is the instrument. The Word is the instrument.

Mr. Wallace: Instrument of the Holy Spirit?

Dr. Stauffer: Yes; can you generate faith without the Word?

Mr. Wallace: No, sir.

Dr. Stauffer: Can you have faith without the Holy Spirit revealing Christ [through the word]?

Mr. Wallace: No, sir.

Dr. Stauffer: Is there anything you have done to get salvation for yourself?

Mr. Wallace: I must repent.

Dr. Stauffer: That is right; but then you won't repent without faith in Christ.

Mr. Wallace: That is right.

Dr. Stauffer: So, don't you see that it isn't anything that you do? You can't repent of yourself, and you have to have the faith in Jesus Christ begotten in you by the Holy Spirit through His Word, and then you accept the salvation which Christ has already purchased by His death and assured to you by His resurrection.

Mr. Wallace: May I ask you a question here? I understood you were starting out to cite instances of infant baptism.

Dr. Stauffer: No—Baptism. I am leading up to it. I want a background. What I am trying to establish now is that you believe in the Bible as the only rule of faith and practice. We believe in salvation through faith and faith alone. I say there are works that you can perform and that I can perform, but they cannot justify or bring salvation because Jesus Christ on the cross made a full salvation for everybody by His death. No man can add to what He has done, so our salvation is through faith alone, and in what Christ has done. If it were not so, I would be putting myself on the same ground right back to the old Catholic teaching of "faith through works." I cannot do anything to win salvation for myself. I say that Jesus Christ, in the teachings of the Bible, by His death, has purchased full and free salvation for all; and that through faith we accept that salvation and become saved through faith in Him. It is not by what you do, my brother, it is not by what I do. If I repent, it is by the grace of God. I am saved by the Grace of God— saved not by works lest any man should boast. If that isn't the work of God, then for centuries somebody has been reading it wrong, and I have been reading it wrong. That is found in Ephesians 2:8-9. "By faith and not by works." All right. You believe in the supreme authority of the Scriptures, and I say our doctrine is that we are saved by faith alone and not by anything that man can add to it. By faith alone. We believe in the supreme authority of the Scriptures—salvation by faith alone, and I suppose you believe also in the right of private judgment?

Mr. Wallace: What do you mean by private judgment?

Dr. Stauffer: I mean that for yourself you must judge His truth for yourself; and you have the same right to do that as I have?

Mr. Wallace: Yes, sir.

Dr. Stauffer: In other words, if there is something on which we agree, that is your right and that is my right. If there is something on which we disagree, that is also your right and my right—the right of private judgment. Therefore, you are not to chide me when I don't see things as you do, and I am not to chide you when you don't understand things as I do. All right. Let me illustrate. In the interpretation of the Scriptures, you cannot avoid the human element. You are as likely to be wrong as I am, and I am as likely to be right as you are. It is the human element entering in. Let me illustrate further. At Cleveland, the Republican Party adopted a platform and when they had adopted it and you could read every word as it was written—yet, they didn't all see it alike. Yet, it was the same thing. When you come to anything that has any human element, that must enter into it. Am I wrong?

Mr. Wallace: Proceed.

Dr. Stauffer: Would you concede that?

Mr. Wallace: I concede that the Scriptures are the authority.

Dr. Stauffer: All right.

Mr. Wallace: And, in my opinion, it doesn't alter the situation or have any bearing on it.

Dr. Stauffer: Yes, it does. When it comes to interpretation of the Scriptures, the human element enters in, and there are, must be, and may be room for differences of opinion, and yet both be honest and see things different.

Mr. Wallace: I concede that we both may be wrong. But we can't both be right, and be different.

Dr. Stauffer: Where any human element enters in, there is a possibility of putting a different interpretation on the same thing. That has been proven from history and not only in relation to religious things but in relation to every other thing. Man hasn't understood things alike and hasn't seen things alike.

When we come to the matter of baptism (and I am stating how our church understands the teachings of the Bible), baptism has been commanded by Jesus Christ—it is His sacrament. It is not simply water, but it is water enjoined in God's command and in connection with God's Word. If it were not in connection with God's word, merely water, it would not be baptism. We believe baptism is not of man. Baptism is of God. It is God's—man is but the instrument to use that which God has instituted. Baptism is a heavenly thing, not an earthly thing. Baptism is not merely water. It is not the person who applies the water, but it is God who bestows the gift that He has promised in baptism.

You recall when Christ spoke to the Jews, where he asked whether the baptism of John was from heaven or of men, and they didn't answer because if they had said from man the multitude would have turned upon them, and if they had said from Heaven, He would have asked "Why don't you believe?" Baptism is not an earthly thing, it is a heavenly thing. If it is without God's Word and without His Promise and without His part in it,—it is merely water and used on the part of a human being, it wouldn't be baptism at all. God commanded baptism and it is a heavenly thing and not an earthly thing. So far as true baptism is concerned, it makes no difference whether the man who performs it is a saint or whether he isn't. Baptism is a thing which Jesus has instituted—it is His own sacrament. We believe that baptism is a sacrament, that it is not only a sign of something that has already been given—it may be that—but that it is an outward sign with an invisible grace. That God has commanded it, and therefore, because He has commanded it, He bestows in and through it what He has promised, the forgiveness of sins.

I want to state what we believe, first, that baptism is not an external thing. That God has instituted it; God has commanded it to be done. That when an individual or any person says that it is nothing but water and a useless thing, we say that it must be exceedingly precious and important. Anything that Christ commanded and instituted must be important. It is not a thing that may be done or left undone—if you are going to be obedient to Christ. I think you would agree with that. And, as I said, to be baptized in the name of God, the Father, Son and Holy Ghost is not to be baptized by man, but by God Himself. And, so, if it is administered at the hand of a man that himself may be evil—if the person who receives the rite of baptism is sincere, that it is baptism and God will bestow His blessing in spite of what the character of the person applying it may be. The efficacy of baptism doesn't depend on my sainthood or my rascality. That doesn't mean that the man who applies it shouldn't be a holy man.

Now then, these are the points I want to impress, all of which we believe are taught in the Bible:

That, taken by itself water is water, but God has connected this water with His Word, and to be baptism you cannot separate His Word from the water. It is God's Word and promise connected with the water, and anything else than that is merely water and nothing more. He honors that water with His name, and He confirms it with His power and authority so that it isn't natural water any more, although it all remains water. It is a heavenly thing, and I want to emphasize that that is the thing that makes baptism efficacious.

It is founded upon God's Word and promise—without that, it is nothing. I may say that the Lutheran faith bases everything on the Word of God. And we believe that the Holy Ghost is present in baptism. That it is He that regenerates, and through Him that the new birth is made possible—"born of water and of the Spirit." That is the purpose of baptism: that we may be saved, and you know that the apostles spoke of baptism for the remission of sins. We, as I say, have baptism in order that we may have the saving grace of God. We don't baptize in order to make a man a prince—to make a man esteemed in the eyes of the world—but to liberate him from sin and death and the devil. Now, simple water couldn't effect that benefit, but with the promise of God—and He is going to be faithful to His promise and to what He has promised, and that is the forgiveness and deliverance from our sins, and from death and the devil.

God's name is in baptism—Father, Son, and Holy Ghost—and where God's name is, there is life and must be salvation. And those who reject baptism reject God's word—reject Father and reject Christ. And we believe in baptism, basing that on the passage which teaches that "He that believes and is baptized shall be saved." It doesn't make any difference, of course, in one sense what we believe about it. You have already expressed something about that. We believe with all our souls that it isn't by works that we are saved. Our works do nothing towards our salvation; but you might say, "Isn't baptism a work?" And I answer as I said before: "Baptism is not our work—it is God's work." The heart must believe.

Well, I think that is our doctrine about baptism. (Dr. Stauffer closes his speech.)

Mr. Wallace: Are you ready for me to talk now?

Dr. Stauffer: Yes.

Mr. Wallace: I would like...

Dr. Stauffer: (interrupting) I don't suppose I have said all I want to on the subject, but I am ready for you.

Mr. Wallace: I suppose you mean this argument to include the question of infant baptism?

Dr. Stauffer: Yes.

Mr. Wallace: This is your statement as to why you believe in infant baptism?

Dr. Stauffer: No. I merely talked about baptism; I will come to infant baptism later on.

Mr. Wallace: Doctor, I wish you would arrive at that—you have been talking over 45 minutes now. The only way we can accomplish anything is in the discussion of our differences.

Dr. Stauffer: All right; I can go on with that. (Resumes his speech,)

I think the thing for us to do is to discuss our agreements and state our positions. I don't care to argue. If, after 1600 years, there have been differences of opinions upon it, and passing down through the centuries that body of people that were known and have been looked upon by Christendom as Christian people, haven't agreed on these things—then you and I or anybody here are not going to solve the problem, and so there is nothing to be gained by our arguing the matter; but as for you stating your faith and I stating mine, that is all right. I don't think you can change me. I came to my position with a great deal of study and prayer, and having arrived, I would have to have more sound arguments than anything that I have ever heard or read to change my opinion.

We believe in the divine instrumentality of the Scriptures. We believe that the Old Testament is as much God's Word as the New Testament, There can be no doubt about that. God inspired the Old as well as the New Testament. It had its place in the plan of God and the salvation of the world; and those things that God has commanded and invoked in the Old Testament and not revoked in the New, are for us today. That the New Testament is not narrower than the Old Covenant; that as much was included in the New Covenant as ever was included in the Old, either in promise or fulfillment.

We believe that when God called Abraham out of the Land in which he lived, He made a covenant with him—a covenant that through him and his people the world should be blessed; and, as a sign and seal of this covenant and of the called people—as a sign, he commanded that the offspring should be circumcised, which was the sign and seal of their having shared in the covenant of Christ which God had promised to Abraham, and that in that covenant children were included as well as adults. The apostles spoke of circumcision taking the place of, or being introduced as circumcision in Christ, which is baptism, showing that it was a parallel in the apostle's mind —that the thing that circumcision did under the Old covenant was done by baptism under the New covenant—the covenant of Christ. On the day of Pentecost, when the Holy Spirit was given Peter said that "the promise is to you and to your children and to them that are afar off."

I also maintain that historical authority (but I don't need to go into that) that the New Testament does not in so many words say you shall baptize infants, but I find that the New Testament nowhere excludes the children which were included under the Old Covenant, and then, I will follow that up by saying that from the days of the apostles down to the present time, there was not a time when infants did not receive baptism. That the Greek Church and the Assyrian Church, which churches are the most closely allied with the early history of the church, have always baptized children. I also affirm that in the early centuries, before the day of the Roman Catholic Church (and don't confuse that because the Greek Assyrian Church and the Greek Catholic Church had little to do with the Roman Catholic Church) baptism of infants was practiced. If you study church history, you well know that. And the statement that is sometimes made that infant baptism wasn't known until the fifteenth century, by the best authorities, cannot be sustained. There never was a time from the days of the apostles to the present that infants were not received into covenant fellowship with Christ by baptism.

My statement is that there is no place in the Bible where it says they should not receive baptism, and that children, infants, were included in the covenant, signed and sealed by the rite of circumcision, and there is no place in the New Testament where it is said children should not have the same right: the seal of the covenant fulfilled with Christ, which is baptism; and I repeat that historical evidence is conclusive that infants were baptized from the days of the apostles. That it was generally practiced might be a question, but that it was practiced, we know. We also have the word of one of the church fathers. (A church father is one who immediately follows, and may have had fellowship in some respect, with the apostles.) That one of them says, "I have received from the apostles that infants should be baptized." So my claim is—our claim is, that there is no period in the church history when infants were not baptized, but I base—we base our statement on the fact that what was included in the Old Testament could not be excluded in the New Testament without a direct command that it should be. And that in the baptism of an infant, it becomes heir to the promise the same as it was to you and to me: that God would bestow His grace upon the children.

That is our reason for baptizing children, and that God has said, "Except a man be born of water and of the spirit, he cannot enter the kingdom of heaven." God has prepared his own instrument through which he has promised to bestow His grace, and we believe that a child never needs to know; and there are many instances in the world when the child never knew the time it wasn't a faithful follower of Jesus Christ—that it never belonged to Satan at any period. And, if I may say so, that is the one thing that led me to the faith that I now hold. The sacredness of the Word of God—I couldn't think that God excluded me as a child from His church, as being a member of His church, a member of His body as a child, so that I got close up in that, and I never need know a time that I wasn't a member of the body of Christ.

(Dr. Stauffer closes his speech.)

MR. WALLACE'S FIRST SPEECH

Mr. Wallace: I want to ask Dr. Stauffer a few questions.

Dr. Stauffer: I will answer to the best of my ability.

Mr. Wallace: 1. Where does the Bible mention infant baptism?

Dr. Stauffer: It does not mention infant baptism, but it does not exclude it.

Mr. Wallace: 2. Does the infant receive any joy and personal obedience in his baptism?

Dr. Stauffer: As that child grows into—

Mr. Wallace: I don't mean as he grows.

Dr. Stauffer: God has promised to bestow His grace. May I ask you a question?

Mr. Wallace: Yes.

Dr. Stauffer: Would you say that God couldn't bestow a blessing upon a child?

Mr. Wallace: I am not questioning what God could do.

Dr. Stauffer: Do you believe that God would bestow a blessing on a child in prayer?

Mr. Wallace: If God had promised that, then the baby would be blest. Does He make such promise?

Dr. Stauffer: I claim that He does bestow grace upon the child, and as it grows into consciousness, it becomes conscious of that blessing.

Mr. Wallace: 3. Is it not practiced without the will of the child, and often against it?

Dr. Stauffer: Yes. No, not often against it. I wouldn't say that.

Mr. Wallace: 4. Do you teach infant baptism comes in the room of circumcision?

Dr. Stauffer: I do. That baptism takes the place of circumcision, because the apostle speaks of the circumcision in Christ, which is baptism.

Mr. Wallace: By what authority do you baptize girl babies?

Dr. Stauffer: You can't do that—I don't know why you would raise that.

Mr. Wallace: I would like for you to answer my question.

Dr. Stauffer: You can make no distinction—all may be baptized.

Mr. Wallace: Would the baptism of a girl baby be in the room of circumcision?

Dr. Stauffer: No, you couldn't very well circumcise girls.

Mr. Wallace: 5. Is there a passage of scripture that teaches that little children born in the "Christian Church" should be baptized?

Dr. Stauffer: No definite passage of scripture which says a child should receive baptism, but there is plenty of scripture to prove that the covenant relationship in God's people belongs to the child as well as to the adult.

Mr. Wallace: 6. Where is the passage (I am asking for scripture) that authorizes the parent to bring the child to baptism?

Dr. Stauffer: There is no definite statement that you, as a parent, shall bring your child in for baptism.

Mr. Wallace: 7. Do the texts that mention household baptisms say that there were babies in those households?

Dr. Stauffer: No, there is no proof of that; no assurance that there were any infants in there, but the probabilities are that where there are five families baptized that there might have been infants who received baptism. That isn't necessary to prove my case.

Mr. Wallace: 8. Is it not possible for a household to exist and there be no children in it?

Dr. Stauffer: Yes.

Mr. Wallace: 9. If the text does not say there were babies in these households, how did you find it out?

Dr. Stauffer: I didn't say there were babies in those households. I said the probabilities were that where five families were baptized, there would be babies, but I didn't affirm there were babies.

Mr. Wallace: You didn't? Isn't it true that you merely assumed there were babies in the households?

Dr. Stauffer: You are asking me something that you have stated as a fact. You are assuming that I said there were infants.

Mr. Wallace: 10. You can deny if you please. Is it not true that you merely assumed the presence of infants in those households?

Dr. Stauffer: I do not assume anything.

Mr. Wallace: You don't assume it. 11. Can an infant believe?

Dr. Stauffer: I am not here to say that an infant does not; certainly, there is no disbelief, and where there is no disbelief there is no objection.

Mr. Wallace: Doctor, I would appreciate it if you would answer my questions. Can an infant believe?

Dr. Stauffer: Not in the sense that an adult can.

Mr. Wallace: 12. Can an infant repent?

Dr. Stauffer: There is no need for repentance where there is no actual sin. It couldn't, no—but you are assuming again that I am asserting something by that question that I haven't said.

Mr. Wallace: I answered your questions direct, and I feel that you ought to answer mine.

Dr. Stauffer: The only thing, Mr. Wallace, is by the questions; by the form of the questions you ask, you assume that I made a declaration that I haven't made.

Mr. Wallace: I am not assuming a thing— I am simply asking you some questions. I answered your questions as you asked them of me. Now, please answer mine. 13. Can an infant confess?

Dr. Stauffer: My questions weren't asked in such a way. I asked you directly if you believed something. The very form of your questions you are asking me, assume that I made such a statement.

Mr. Wallace: Of course, it you are afraid to answer—

Dr. Stauffer: No, sir; I don't think—

Mr. Wallace: Can an infant confess?

Dr. Stauffer: There is nothing to be confessed.

Mr. Wallace: Can he confess?

Dr. Stauffer: No.

Mr. Wallace: 14. Can an infant receive the Word of God?

Dr. Stauffer: Yes, as he grows into consciousness.

Mr. Wallace: As an infant?

Dr. Stauffer: It can receive—yes, it can receive the sacramental Word of God.

Mr. Wallace: I don't mean the sacramental Word of God.

Dr. Stauffer: Yes, it can receive the Word of God—God's word is His promise.

Mr. Wallace: 15. Can an infant continue steadfastly in the apostle's doctrine, in fellowship, in the breaking of bread, and in prayer?

Dr. Stauffer: Not as an infant.

Mr. Wallace: 16. Can an infant be taught?

Dr. Stauffer: Yes, sir.

Mr. Wallace: 17. If there was ever a baby baptized in the New Testament times, who baptized it? Was it Peter, Paul, Luke, or who?

Dr. Stauffer: How would I know who did it?

Mr. Wallace: 18. Whose baby was it?

Dr. Stauffer: How should I know?

Mr. Wallace: 19. Where was it done? In Jerusalem? Corinth? Rome? or where?

Dr. Stauffer: Well, I am sure at different places. It doesn't say, but we have the historical statement of men who were in touch with men of that time that infants were baptized.

Mr. Wallace: I am concerned only with the New Testament. Where was it done?

Dr. Stauffer: Oh, that is not material. I can't tell you where it was done.

Mr. Wallace: 20. When was it done?

Dr. Stauffer: Infants were baptized in the days of the apostles and on through all the centuries of the church.

Mr. Wallace: 21. How was it done?

Dr. Stauffer: Well, in some instances it was done by plunging the child info the water, and in other times it was done by applying the water to the child.

Mr. Wallace: 22. Why was it done?

Dr. Stauffer: Excepting a man be born of water and the Spirit, he cannot enter the kingdom of heaven.

Mr. Wallace: I would like now to make a few observations. I appreciate this invitation to come here today and discuss with you what the Bible teaches. My motive is simply for truth. The truth has all to gain and nothing to lose.

I am not concerned about what history teaches, except Divine History—the history recorded in the Bible. The Doctor and I agree that the Bible is the supreme authority; that being the authority, the supreme authority, on it we should rely, and we do not need to turn to what some man has said. The thing that has confused people today is what man has said.

Now, in regard to baptism, there are a few things said by our friend, Dr. Stauffer, that I would like to notice. He first talks about the evidence of man's history, as it were, about which I am not the slightest concerned. He talks about baptism being an outward sign, of some inward token, but fails to cite a text as proof thereof. He raised the question—

Dr. Stauffer: (interrupting) May I just stop you there? I said that baptism was the outward sign with the invisible grace; that God, in baptism, has promised the forgiveness of sins. You have read that.

Mr. Wallace: You simply mean by that, that baptism is for the remission of sins?

Dr. Stauffer: I believe that when we receive baptism, God will honor His own sacrament and do what He has promised.

Mr. Wallace: We teach that baptism is for the remission of sins.

Dr. Stauffer: We agree on that, and that remission of sins is a divine grace bestowed; isn't it?

Mr. Wallace: The remission of sins comes as a result of obedience to Christ. Baptism is for the remission of sins to the penitent believer.

As I was saying, he raised the question of the administrator in baptism. With him, on this topic, we hold no controversy.

In regard to justification by faith, he brings that up, there are a few things that I would like to say. First of all, let us notice how faith comes.

We teach that faith comes by hearing the word of God, because that is the way the Bible teaches it. In Acts 15:7-9, we read: "And when there had been much questioning, Peter rose up and said unto them, Brethren, ye know that a good while ago, God made choice among you that by my mouth the Gentiles should hear the word of the gospel and believe." So we see that faith came to the Gentiles by hearing the word of the gospel. Again, in Acts 18:8, we are told that "Crispus, the ruler of the Synagogue, believed in the Lord with all his house; and many of the Corinthians, hearing, believed, and were baptized." The Corinthians heard before they believed. In John's gospel, chapter 17, verse 20, Jesus said: "Neither for these only do I pray, but for them also that believe on me through their word." Our Lord taught here that faith came by the word of the apostles. Again we read: "Many other signs, therefore, did Jesus in the presence of his disciples which are not written in this book: but these are written that you may believe that Jesus is the Christ, the Son of God, and that believing ye may have life in his name." (John 20:30-31). To settle this matter beyond controversy, we simply read a statement from Paul in Romans 10:17, "So then faith cometh by hearing and hearing by the word of God."

Now, we recognize and teach that the Holy Spirit operates in conversion. We do not question that. The question is: How does He operate in conversion? We affirm that the Bible is the medium through which He works in conversion. And as to this, if I understand the Doctor correctly, we agree. Jesus said, in Matthew 10:20, "For it is not ye that speak, but the Spirit of my Father that speaketh in you." The word of God is the medium through which God speaks to the hearts of men and women today.

The Bible is not the Holy Spirit. Paper and ink are not the Holy Spirit. The Bible is simply the Word of God recorded by ink on paper. The power is in the divine intelligence, communicated through signs of ideas, in ink on paper. This is not God (holding up the Bible). This is not Christ. This is not the Holy Spirit. This Book contains the Words of God, of Christ, and of the Holy Spirit. Without the hearing of these Words, there can be no faith.

When it comes to the question of justification by faith, we believe that a man is saved by faith. The question is: When is he saved by faith? Dr. Stauffer admits that there is not a single text that says we are saved by faith only. The passage to which he referred does not say we are saved by faith only. Paul says: "Being, therefore, justified by faith, we have peace with God through our Lord Jesus Christ." (Rom. 5:1.) Paul did not say "faith only." In fact, James says: "Ye see then how that by works a man is justified and *not* by faith only." Faith only is mentioned once in the Bible and God said: "Not by faith only." The Doctor says justification is by faith only, and James says it is not. I had rather take what James says, as he was inspired.

Understand me: We do not teach that works, such as James speaks of, are meritorious works, as the Catholics speak of. We say that in order for a man to be saved, he must be obedient. "Not every one that sayeth unto me Lord, Lord, shall enter into the Kingdom of heaven; but he that DOETH THE WILL of my Father who is heaven." (Matt. 7:21.) "Everyone, therefore, that heareth these words of mine and DOETH them, shall be likened unto a wise man." (Matt. 7:24.) The passage mentioned by Dr. Stauffer in Ephesians does not teach against obedience. When Paul in Ephesians 2:8-9 says, "Not of works," he was not speaking about the works of obedience but the "works" of the Mosaic Law. In Romans 3:27, Paul shows that the "works'" about which one could boast was excluded. "Where is boasting, then? It is excluded. By what law; of works? Nay; but by the law of faith." The law of faith excludes boasting, but does not exclude obedience.

When Paul says, "Not of works" he did not mean not of obedience, as he himself said, "Know ye not that to whom ye present yourselves as servants unto obedience, his servants ye are whom ye obey." (Rom. 6:16.)

In order to further establish the fact that one is not justified by "faith only," I call your attention to the following:

1. If a man is saved by faith only, he is saved without the new birth. In John 1:12, we read: "But as many as received him, to them gave he the right to become children of God." From this we see that one may be a believer and not be a child of God. For the believer is given the right to become the child of God. Believers are given the right to become the children of God. If one is saved the moment he believes, he is saved before he exercises his right to become a child of God. If then he is saved the moment he believes, he is saved before he becomes a child of God, and if saved before he becomes a child of God, he is saved without the new birth, for one cannot be born anew without in the new birth becoming a child of God. The doctrine of justification by faith only nullifies the new birth.

Dr. Stauffer: (interrupting) I would like to have you make that statement again— if we are saved by faith only.

Mr. Wallace: As many as received Him, to them gave He the power to become sons of God, even to them that believe on His name. Believers are given the right to become the children of God.

Mrs. Maack: (interrupting) How do you get that statement, saved without the new birth?

Mr. Wallace: (ignoring Mrs. Maack's question, continues his statement to Dr. Stauffer) Furthermore, if one is saved the moment he believes, he is saved before he becomes a child of God because the believer is given the right *to become* a child of God.

2. If one is saved by faith only, he is saved by an imperfect faith. "Was not Abraham our father justified by works, in that he offered up Isaac his son upon the altar? Thou seest that faith wrought with his works, and by works was faith made perfect" (James 2:21-22.) Faith must exist before it works. It must work before it is perfected. If one is saved by faith only he is saved by an imperfect faith.

3. If one is saved by faith only, he is saved by dead faith. "For as the body apart from the spirit is dead, even so faith apart from works is dead." (James 2:26.) "Even so, faith, if it have not works, is dead in itself." (James 2:17.) Since it is impossible to be saved by dead faith, it is impossible to be saved by faith alone.

4. If one can be saved by faith alone, he can be saved without confessing the name of Christ. "Nevertheless, even of the rulers many believed on him; but because of the Pharisees they did not confess it, lest they should be put out of the synagogue: for they loved the glory that is of men more than the glory that is of God." (John 12:42-43.) Please notice that these rulers believed ON Christ. Their faith was a dead faith, an imperfect faith. In order to be saved by faith, one must obey. Faith must exercise the believer. What I mean by this can be ascertained from the record in Acts and Romans. Luke says, "And a great company of the priests were obedient to the faith." (Acts 6:7). In Romans 1:5 and 16:26, we read about the "obedience of faith." Then, if one can be saved by faith only, he can:

a. Be saved without confessing Christ. (Jesus teaches that this is impossible—Matt. 10:32-33.)

b. Be saved and at the same time love man more than he loves God. (Will God save a man that loves men better than he loves God, and is too cowardly to confess Jesus Christ? These men had faith only.)

Dr. Stauffer: (interrupting) May I come back to Abraham? Did he do his work in offering up Isaac in order to be justified, or was it in carrying out a faith which was already there which he had and which if he was going to maintain, must require obedience? You see what I mean —it was the works that follow faith rather than the two going together. In other words, his works were the acknowledgment of his faith: and he showed his faith by the fact that he was willing to offer Isaac.

Mr. Wallace: By faith, Abraham offered up his son Isaac—

Mrs. Maack: (interrupting) Before he had the faith.

Mr. Wallace: (ignoring Mrs. Maack, continued his answer to Dr. Stauffer) James says the faith WROUGHT WITH HIS WORKS. Paul says Abraham OBEYED by faith (Heb. 11:8).

5. The Bible teaches that faith only will not avail. "For in Christ Jesus neither circumcision availeth anything, nor uncircumcision, but faith working through love." (Gal. 5:6).

a. Faith must exist before it works.

b. It must work before it avails.

c. It avails when it works.

Thus we see that faith only will not avail, or save, as it must work before it avails.

Mrs. Maack: (interrupting: What would you offer these little children, conceived and born in sin? Born in the line of Adam?

Mr. Wallace: Will you kindly wait a minute—I will come to that.

Mrs. Maack: Well, if I can.

Mr. Wallace: We say that justification is by faith, but not by faith only. Look how the writer in Hebrews uses the phrase "by faith." By faith, Noah built the ark. By faith Abraham obeyed. By faith, the children of Israel crossed the Red Sea, The ark was not built by faith only, neither did the children of Israel cross the Red Sea by faith only. So, then, justification by faith simply means taking God at His word and doing what He says.

Now, taking up the question of infant baptism. You account for this because of Church History—that historians from early days mentioned it. I care not what they mentioned. You can prove anything by church history for the simple reason that among different religious bodies, people have written histories. What I am concerned about is: What does the Bible teach. You may find where some historian mentioned infant baptism, but you can't find where the text mentions it.

Dr. Stauffer: (interrupting) Now, let me stop you there. I said, before I spoke anything at all about historical matters, that history was supplemental, that we based our faith on the fact that infants were included in the covenant under the Old Dispensation, and it has never been revoked. There is no place in the Bible which says that infants are not to be baptized. I want to make that statement.

Mr. Wallace: He says history is supplemental. I maintain that the Bible does not mention infant baptism and care nothing about what history says.

Dr. Stauffer: (interrupting) I don't know why you want to make statements as though you felt that I had made a certain statement. You infer that our reason for infant baptism is because it is historical.

Mr. Wallace: Well, why did you bring history into this?

Dr. Stauffer: I brought it up—you know what for—supplementary evidence. We find that nowhere in the Bible have children been excluded from the right of the covenant— which is baptism.

Mr. Wallace: We, as members of the Body of Christ, are governed by what the Bible says, and not by what it does not say.

(At this point, there was so much confusion that it was impossible to get all that was said. Dr. Stauffer and Mrs. Maack were both talking at once. Mr. Wallace asked Dr. Stauffer and Mrs. Maack to please talk one at a time.)

Mrs. Maack: This isn't a heated discussion. There is no need to be so excited.

Mr. Wallace: You are the one that is excited, dear sister; if not, then please be quiet.

Mrs. Maack: When a question comes up, I want it answered.

Mr. Wallace: Will you please let me proceed. I will answer your question concerning the babies when I come to it. I am following Dr. Stauffer, and I have made a notation of the question you raised and will reply to it in due time,

Mr. Herrington: I would like to ask—

Mr. Wallace: Bro. Herrington, you will please leave the discussion to me.

Mrs. Maack: Jesus wasn't born under the line of Adam.

Mr. Wallace: Mrs. Maack, won't you please let me finish my argument on infant baptism?

Mrs. Maack: No, I won't. That is what we came here for. I came in here to find out what I want to know.

Mr. Wallace: Dr. Stauffer, I have asked you folks to let me proceed with my statement. I sat here and listened to all you had to say. Today, I am here as your guest and I think that in all common courtesy I ought to be heard without being disturbed so much. I have elected my own order of rebuttal, and will reply to these things as I come to them.

Dr. Stauffer: Let him proceed.

Mr. Wallace: As I was saying: We as people are not governed by what the Book does not say. The Bible doesn't say, "Thou shalt not have a Pope." It does not say that we shall not count beads or burn incense. It does not say, "Thou shalt not kiss the Pope's big toe." The Bible tells us WHAT to do. "Every scripture inspired of God is also profitable for teaching, for reproof, for correction, for instruction which is in righteousness: that the man of God may be complete, furnished completely unto every good work" (II Tim. 3:16-17.) This Book (holding up the Bible) furnishes completely everything God wants us to do. Nowhere does it mention infant baptism.

I maintain that the Bible excludes infant baptism. This I will show very shortly. My objections to infant baptism are based upon the following points:

1. The Bible does not mention it. He says that the Bible does not mention it, but does not exclude it. I have shown you that by that rule many things could be brought in. Again I say, we are governed by what the Book *says* and not by what it does *not* say.

2. Infant baptism robs the individual of the joy of personal obedience. The Doctor says he receives joy as he grows, yet that is not what I asked. Even when one grows, he could have no joy "of personal obedience" because it was not a personal act. How could an unconscious infant receive personal joy? As you know, "personal joy" is due to "personal obedience." How could an infant receive any joy of personal obedience about something he does not know anything on earth about?

3. Infant baptism is practiced without the will of the child and often against it. Never does an unconscious baby give its consent to be baptized.

4. Dr. Stauffer teaches it comes in the room of circumcision. For this he could not cite a text. At the same time, he says this: He knows that only male children could be circumcised. Shame on the man that stands up in the name of Christ to baptize girl babies in the room of circumcision. Even if we were to admit that baptism of infants comes in the room of circumcision there would be no authority for baptizing girl babies. That which proves too much, proves nothing; therefore, the Doctor's argument on circumcision does not prove anything.

5. There is no passage of scripture that teaches that children, born in the "Christian Church" (that is, born in families that are members of the church), should be baptized. This our friend admits.

6. Parents are not authorized to bring their children to baptism. I asked the Doctor for such passage and he replied, "There is no definite statement that you, as a parent, should bring your child in for baptism." Why, then, do they do it? They have no authority to do so.

7. Infant baptism based upon the household baptisms recorded in the Bible, rests upon a mere assumption. I asked if the texts that mention household baptisms say there were babies in those households. To this, he replies, "There is no proof of it." There is "no assurance" that infants were in those households. He admits that a household may exist and there be no babies in it, yet he says the "probabilities were that where five families were baptized, there would be babies." So, you see the household baptisms furnish no proof. There is no "proof," no "assurance" and it rests only upon a "probability." Again, I asked, "Is it not true that you merely assumed the presence of infants in those households?" He replies, "I don't assume anything." They were "probably there." The word "probably" is an assumption within itself.

8. Faith must precede baptism and infants cannot believe; therefore, they are not subjects of baptism (Heb. 11:6.) "Faith comes by hearing and hearing by the word of God." (Rom. 10:17). He admits, or says, an infant cannot believe.

Dr. Stauffer: (interrupting) No, I didn't say it that way. I said there was no evidence of unbelief present.

Mr. Wallace: (continuing) There can be no unbelief and at the same time be no faith. An infant can neither believe nor disbelieve. To believe it would have to "receive the evidence" and to disbelieve it would have to "reject the evidence." A baby can do neither.

9. Only those who confess are subjects of baptism. Infants cannot confess, therefore they are not subjects of baptism. (Acts 8:37). He frankly admits that an infant cannot confess. Since only those who confess are to be baptized, and infants cannot confess, they are not subjects of baptism.

10. Repentance must precede baptism and infants cannot repent; therefore, they are not to be baptized (Acts 2:38). Our friend admits they cannot repent.

11. Only those who receive the word were baptized (Acts 2:41). Infants cannot receive the word of God.

12. Those who were baptized continued steadfastly in the apostles' doctrine, the breaking of bread, and prayer (Acts 2: 42). The Doctor admits that an infant cannot do this.

I asked the Doctor if there was ever a baby baptized in New Testament times, and he "does not know." Whose baby was it? He did not know. Where was it done? He did not know. When was it done? He tells about history. I am concerned only about what the Bible says. How was it done? He tells about different ways in which it was done, but could not cite a text. Why was it done? He cited John 3:5. If this applies to infants, then the child that is not baptized cannot enter into the kingdom of God. Tell us what becomes of the unbaptized babies. "Except one be born of water and the spirit, he cannot enter into the kingdom of God." If this applies to babies, please tell us what becomes of the unbaptized babies?

Dr. Stauffer: (interrupting) What would you say becomes of it?

Mr. Wallace: Doctor, the infant is SAFE.

13. The Bible teaches that infants are subjects of the kingdom of heaven (Matt. 19:14): "Suffer the little children to come unto me and forbid them not, for to such belongeth the kingdom of God." Jesus says the kingdom of God belongs to the little child. In this connection, Mrs. Maack, I will answer your question. You want to know, that, if a child born in the line of Adam is sinful? May I ask, where is the text that says a child is born a sinner?

Mrs. Maack: I can't give it; Dr. Stauffer can.

Dr. Stauffer: "For as in Adam all die, even so in Christ shall all be made alive."

Mr. Wallace: You mean to tell me, Doctor, you can't cite me a text that says that babies are born in sin?

Dr. Stauffer: All are born in sin—conceived and born in sin. Psalms 51:5.

Mr. Wallace: The passage the Doctor refers to in 1st Corinthians teaches that all we lost unconditionally in Adam we gain unconditionally in Christ (I Cor. 15:22). We suffer the consequences of the sin of Adam, but not the guilt. Sin cannot be transmitted from parent to child. The very definition of sin proves this: "Sin is the transgression of the law" (I John 3:4). The father kills someone—thus he sins. This was an ACT, and the child is not guilty of the ACT. The child may approve the act and be punished for the wicked approval, but not the ACT. He may suffer the consequence of the act—be made an orphan—if the State takes his father's life to pay for the crime; but, he is not guilty of the sin. As a consequence of the sin of Adam we all die a natural death. A physical death. As a result of the resurrection of Christ, we will all be raised from the dead. Our bodies die as the consequence of the sin of Adam and our bodies will be raised as a consequence of the resurrection of our Lord.

Psalms 51:5 does not say that a child is born in sin. It says: "Behold, I was brought forth in iniquity, and in sin did my mother conceive me." However, may I say if inherent sin comes from the mother (and Jesus was born of woman) that makes Him a sinner. If inherent sin comes from the mother, you make Jesus a sinner; but, if you say it comes from the father, this text does not apply as nothing is said about the father.

But, may I ask: Does inherent sin come from the flesh or from the spirit? If you say it comes from the flesh, you make Jesus a sinner, for He was born of the flesh. If you say it comes from the spirit, you make God a sinner as He is the father of our spirits (Heb. 12:9). You may take either horn of the dilemma you may choose, and yet by this doctrine you either make Jesus Christ or God Almighty a sinner.

The child is safe. It is not lost. Jesus came to seek and to save that which is lost. Our Lord said, speaking of children, "to such belongeth the kingdom of God."

14. The covenant under which we live is not the OLD covenant continued, but it is a NEW covenant. The church of Christ is not the church that was in the wilderness. Paul calls the church a NEW MAN (Eph. 2:15). All who enter this New Covenant must know the Lord before they enter (Heb. 8:11). The Jews came into the Old covenant by a natural birth and were taught to know the Lord as they grew up. In the New covenant, "They shall not teach every man his fellow-citizen, and every man his brother, saying: Know the Lord, for all shall know me, from the least to the greatest." In the New covenant, all know the Lord from the least to the greatest.

Dr. Stauffer says, "That God made a covenant with the children of Israel and in that covenant He included children. The Law of Circumcision given to Abraham was made a part of the covenant given to Israel, and that baptism came into the room of circumcision." But does he not know that circumcision was given to Abraham as a sign and seal of his faith? (Rom. 4:11). Given as a sign and seal of the faith he already had. When you baptize an infant, is it done as a sign and seal of the faith it already has?

He argues that the covenant under which we live is the same one under which the Jews lived. Paul says, "If the first covenant had been found faultless, then no place would have been sought for a second. For, finding fault with them, he said: Behold the days cometh, said the Lord, that I will make a new covenant with the house of Israel and with the house of Judah; not according to the covenant that I made with their fathers, in the day that I took them by the hand to lead them out of Egypt" (Heb. 8:7-9). Doctor, there is the fallacy in your statement. Paul says we have a covenant NOT ACCORDING to the covenant made with "their fathers." The whole argument based upon the old covenant has no bearing whatsoever, because Paul says we have a covenant not according to the covenant made with their fathers. The Doctor says it is according to the old covenant. The old covenant was abolished (Col. 2:14). We are not under it (Rom. 6:15). We became dead to it (Rom. 7:4). We are discharged from it (Rom. 6:7). It is done away in Christ (II Cor. 3:14). We do not live under a continuation of the old covenant. Paul says it is a NEW covenant.

[The following exchange was added in writing during the proofreading of the original publication, and were not part of the original discussion]

Dr. Stauffer: I say the Old Covenant included children—The New does not exclude them—I did not say it was the same. You are unfair in that you make me to say what I did not say.

Mr. Wallace: I did not deny that the New Covenant makes provisions for the infant. Jesus said, "To such belongs the Kingdom of God." The provision for the infant is made without the condition of baptism. The Doctor's argument would exclude from the home of the soul all babies who are not baptized. I showed that the New Covenant does exclude "infant baptism" and that the infant is SAFE and needs no baptism.

The Dr. seems to forget his own statements. On page 22, of his first speech where he makes the argument on circumcision and the covenants, to try to bring infant baptism into the New Covenant he says, "The apostles spoke of circumcision taking the place of, or being introduced as circumcision in Christ, which is baptism, showing that it WAS PARALLEL in the apostle's mind—that the thing circumcision did under the OLD LAW was done by baptism under the NEW." So he argues there is a parallel between the two laws. Webster defines parallel as being, "Like in essential parts and characteristics; as parallel passages." I showed clearly that there is no parallel between the Covenants and the New Covenant was a "NEW" Covenant in every respect. Baptism does not come in the room of anything. It is a NEW ordinance in a NEW Covenant.

[End of additional notes]

Again he bases his authority for infant baptism upon the promise and covenant God made with Abraham. God did not make a covenant with Abraham in the day that He brought him out of the Land of Ur. In this passage (Gen. 12:1-3), there are two distinct promises but no covenant. 1—There is the land promise. 2—There is the spiritual promise—that all nations would be blessed through His seed. This land promise became a covenant (Gen. 17:13). It was a covenant in the FLESH (Gen. 17:13). It is true that this covenant included circumcision, but the church of Christ did not come of the Covenant. It came of the promise. Circumcision was not in the promise, and since the Lord's church came of the promise it could not have fleshly circumcision, nor anything to come in the room thereof. Paul teaches that the church came of the promise and not of the law, that is, the old covenant (Gal. 3:15-18). The law which came four hundred and thirty years after did not nullify the promise. Our inheritance is of the promise and not of the law— the old covenant (Gal. 3:18).

15. We see that infants are not to be baptized, because baptism is to the believer. An infant cannot believe. Teaching must precede baptism. An infant cannot be taught. Baptism follows a confession of faith. Infants cannot confess. Infant baptism is done in the name of our Heavenly Father, but He does not require it. It is done in the name of Christ, but He never taught it. It is done in the name of the Holy Spirit, but He never authorized it. Jesus says the little child belongs to the kingdom of God. "Except ye turn and become as little children, ye shall in no wise enter into the kingdom of God." (Matt. 18:3.) Did He mean to teach that except ye be converted and become little sinners, you could not enter the kingdom of God?

The Record on Baptism

To show that infants are not subjects of baptism we only need to look at the record. The record of those whom the apostles baptized proves who are the subjects of baptism.

1. Acts 2:41: "Then they that received the word were baptized." Not an infant in this number for they received the word of God. Infants cannot receive the word of God.

2. Acts 8:12: "They were baptized, both men and women." No infant here.

3. Acts 8:28-39: The eunuch—one man. No infant here.

4. Acts 9:18: Saul of Tarsus. No infant here.

5. Acts 10:48: Cornelius—one man. If it be argued that the household of Cornelius was baptized, please remember this: The Book says "And he (Peter) COMMANDED them to be baptized." Infants cannot receive a command, therefore no infants were

baptized. All who were baptized were commanded to be baptized.

6. Acts 16:15: Lydia and her household, In verse 13, we read that Paul spake unto the WOMEN that were come together. "And they (Paul and Silas) went out of the prison and entered the house of Lydia: and when they had seen the brethren, they comforted them." All in the household of Lydia were old enough to be comforted by Paul and Silas. There were no infants because all in the household were comforted by the teaching of Paul and Silas.

7. Acts 16: The jailor. No infant here, as may be seen by reading verse 34: "And when he had brought them into his house, he sat meat before them and rejoiced, believing in God with ALL his house." All in his house were old enough to believe.

8. Acts 18: The Corinthians and Crispus, the ruler of the Synagogue. "Crispus, the chief ruler of the synagogue, believed on the Lord with ALL his house; and many of the Corinthians HEARING, BELIEVED, and were baptized." ALL in the household of Crispus were old enough to believe and the Corinthians HEARD and BELIEVED. Babies cannot hear the gospel and believe, therefore there were no infants in this number.

9. Acts 19:1-5: Twelve MEN were baptized. Not an infant here.

Thus we see that out of the entire number baptized by the apostles, there is not an infant included. There is not a single command nor example for infant baptism in all the Bible. The doctrine of infant baptism is not once mentioned in the Word of God. Can you, my friends, believe it is your duty to do in the name of Christ that which He never authorized?

Mrs. Maack: Suppose a baby isn't supposed to be baptized; if we took the baby and had it baptized, what wrong are we doing?

Mr. Wallace: Paul says in Romans 14:23, that "whatsoever is not of faith, is sin." "Faith comes by hearing and hearing by the word of

God." The word of God does not authorize it and when you do something the Word does not authorize, it is sin.

This final appeal to the Book shows that infant baptism is excluded:

1. In II Peter 1:3, the Book says, "His divine power hath granted us all things that pertain to life and godliness." He has not given us infant baptism, therefore it does not pertain unto life and godliness.

2. Peter says that baptism is an answer of a good conscience (I Pet. 3:21). The unconscious infant cannot have a good conscience, therefore it cannot be baptized.

3. Christ told the apostles that the Spirit would "guide them into ALL truth." The Holy Spirit did not guide them into the practice of infant baptism, therefore it is not of the truth of God. Jesus also said, that the "Holy Spirit will bring all things to your remembrance, whatsoever I have said unto you." The Holy Spirit did not one time bring to their remembrance a command to baptize infants, therefore Christ did not command it.

4. "Whatsoever goeth onward and abideth not in the teaching of Christ, hath not God. (II John 9). Infant baptism is not in the teaching of Christ and he who practices it is not abiding in the teachings of Christ. Since those who practice infant baptism do not abide in the teaching of Christ, they have not God. This is what John says, and it is TRUE.

We have seen that there is not a single case of infant baptism in the Bible. The Bible does not teach it, does not mention it. We have seen that all cases of baptism were those who were able to believe, to be taught, and to repent. They were old enough to understand. We have seen that Jesus said that the kingdom belongs to little children. The gospel is to those who can be taught. "Go teach all nations," said Jesus, "baptizing them." We do not baptize nations as such, we baptize the taught of the nations. The subject of baptism is one who is old enough to be taught—and we are governed by what the BOOK

SAYS, and not by what it does NOT say.

DR. STAUFFER'S REBUTTAL SPEECH

To maintain that there were no children in Lydia's household because they were comforted, is ridiculous. Why, in my father's house, my brothers had all kinds of children, and people would come there and hold services and they were comforted. It is a ridiculous statement, and, anyway, you are maintaining something that I did not say. I said there were probably infants in those households. Because they were comforted does not prove that there weren't infants in the house.

He says, "The Bible is addressed to intelligence. There is not a word addressed to an eight-day-old baby." He is giving the same argument they always do. They argue everything said in the Bible to children is said to the adult. I can prove on that basis a child is lost. "He that believeth and is baptized, shall be saved; but he that believeth not, shall be damned." If a child is not baptized, then it is damned. "He that believeth not shall be damned." Therefore, a child cannot believe, and, therefore, it is damned.

A child is born in iniquity and sin. If the sin of Adam was not visited upon the children—is not in the child—how is it that there have never been any children that have grown up and been free of sin? If the roots of the nature is not in there—because a person acts according to its nature—why should there be sin there at all?

If there is not sinful nature in the child—if that which is contrary to God is not inherent in the child's nature—will you tell me why it is that in all history and in all knowledge of the human race there never has been a child that hasn't shown that it has sin, that which we say is the sin that comes from Adam, in its character. How is it in all the world there has never been a child who, born sinless, has been free from sin. I don't say that an infant has committed any actual sin. I mean of a sinful nature—that which is contrary to God and His image in which God originally made man—that nature within the child, the same as in Adam, if he cannot sin. As in Adam, all have sinned. There is no difference. A child is a child of Satan. An infant is a child of Adam. Why is it if a child is not sinful and does not have a sinful nature that in all history of the human race there has never been one which has grown into manhood free of it? WHY? (Rom. 3:9-18; Eph. 2:3.)

You are going on to deny that out of that have grown these things. How can you get a thing out—if it is not within its nature? Everything acts according to its nature. If you plant a pear tree, you get pears— nothing else. The reason a child does that which is wrong and shows that sinful nature is because it grows out of a degenerate nature. All history and all experience proves a child has within it the original nature which separates it from God, and is sinful, and out of that grows these sinful acts spoken of in Rom. 3:8-18.

You mean to say then there was no need for a child to have Christ die for it? You say a child would go to heaven if Jesus had never died? Jesus died for all sinners and a child is sinful. The sins of the fathers shall be visited on the children in the third and fourth generation (Ex. 20:5).

MR. WALLACE'S REBUTTAL SPEECH

There could not have been infants in the household of Lydia as the text says Paul and Silas entered into the house of Lydia and when they had seen the brethren they comforted them. There were not children because it says they comforted them. This shows that by the teaching of Paul and Silas they were comforted. You can't comfort infants by preaching—yet, the household of Lydia was thus comforted, therefore, there were no infants in her household. If there were infants in this household and infants cannot be comforted by preaching, how do you suppose Paul and Silas comforted these babies? Did Paul walk the floor with a little fellow and jiggle him up and down while Silas warmed the baby's bottle? Paul was not a baby nurse. He was a gospel preacher and the comfort he brought to the house of Lydia was by preaching the word. All in her house were old enough to hear the word.

The Bible was addressed to intelligence. There is not a word addressed to a baby. Your effort to prove babies will be lost, if they are not to be taught, by using the passage which says: "He that believeth and is baptized, shall be saved; but he that believeth not, shall be damned," does you no good. The expression "He that beliveth not," has reference to one who rejects the gospel. A baby does not reject the gospel. This can be seen by reading the Revised Version, which you accept, and it says, "He that disbelieveth shall be condemned," A baby does not disbelieve. It is your doctrine, Doctor, that involves infant damnation. If John 3:5, as you say, applies to the baby, tell us what becomes of the unbaptized baby? "Except ye be born of water and the Spirit ye cannot enter the kingdom of God." If a child cannot enter the kingdom of God without baptism, then all unbaptized babies will be excluded from the kingdom of God. The truth is, however, John 3:5 has no reference to infants. Of infants, Jesus says: "To such belongeth the kingdom of God." A baby would go to heaven even if Jesus had never died. Jesus died for the lost. Babies are not lost. They are SAFE.

The nature of the child seems to worry the Doctor. Why is it, he says, that they will all sin, if they do not have a sinful nature? I do not deny that the child has the power of choice. The power of choice is not evil. We become sinners, when, by that power of choice, we choose evil. He wants to know why it is that no one has ever grown into manhood free from sin, if a baby is not born in sin? Here is your example. Jesus was born of the flesh—his flesh came from the line of Adam and He grew into manhood without sin. The reason Jesus did not sin was because He did not yield to temptation—"He was tempted in all points" even as we are tempted.

However, the doctrine of our friend is the teaching that presents the puzzle. You infer, that if a child is born pure and sinless that it would grow to manhood without sin. Now, may I ask, since you baptize a baby to wash away the Adamic sin—when that sin is washed away it has no sin, as you say, it has no ACTUAL, sin—why is it that Lutheran children do not grow up without ever sinning? WHY? You know. There is no difference in the action of the baptized and of the unbaptized baby.

The texts cited by the Doctor do not prove his points. Romans Three does not say they were born sinful. It says, "They have all turned... become...used tongues for deceit...mouth full of cursing and bitterness." They were not born sinful—they turned and became sinful.

In Ephesians 2:1-3, there is nothing said about the infant. These brethren were guilty of sin, but not Adam's sin. They were guilty of *their* trespasses and sins—not Adam's sins. The condition from which they were redeemed was one in which they once walked—not born. They were by nature—not birth—the children of wrath.

Paul says in I Cor. 11:14, "Doth not even nature itself teach you, that if a man have long hair it is a dishonor to him?" The nature spoken of here is the custom or practice and not birth. These people were by nature, custom, practice, the children of wrath. The context makes this clear for it says, "We once lived in the lusts of our flesh, doing the desires of the flesh."

"The sins of the fathers shall be visited upon the third and fourth generation." This does not apply to inherent sins; if so, it would play out in the third or fourth generation. PHYSICAL AND MENTAL WEAKNESS COMES FROM THE FLESH AND MAY BE THE CONSEQUENCE OF SIN BUT NOT THE GUILT.

God once destroyed this world with water. The earth was repopulated from eight righteous souls. If these were righteous, and the text says they were, how did this inherent sin get started again?

Ezekiel says, "Yet say ye, wherefore doth not the son bear the iniquity of the father?...THE SON SHALL NOT BEAR THE INIQUITY OF THE FATHER."

[The following exchange was added during proofreading, and was not part of the original discussion]

Dr. Stauffer: We do not believe, nor do we teach, that a baby unbaptized is lost. That question was not discussed. You infer that because we believe it is the will of God that infants should be baptized—and that in baptism they receive the new life, that consequently the unbaptized child is lost, and that is not the case.

Mr. Wallace: Yes, Doctor the question was discussed. On page 49, of your rebuttal speech you will find that you raised the question yourself. Here are your own words: "I can prove on that basis a child is lost." Then you strive to press what you believe the consequence of Mark 16:15, 16. In your effort, though, you found the dart to be fatal to yourself. I showed the truth of God's word and then proved beyond a doubt, that your doctrine, whether you believe it or not, involves infant damnation. Instead of all this complaining why did not you answer my question found on page 52, of my rebuttal, which says, "If John 3:5 applies to the baby as you say, TELL US WHAT BECOMES OF THE UNBAPTIZED BABY?" Jesus says without this new birth one CANNOT enter the kingdom of God. If this applies to babies then the unbaptized baby will be lost. If the unbaptized baby will not be lost then this does not apply to babies. Instead of writing down an objection to what I said, why did you not answer this question: "What will become of the unbaptized baby?"

[End of added material]

THE LORD'S SUPPER

At this point, Dr. Stauffer suggested that Mr. Wallace go ahead and state what he believes about the Lord's Supper. Mr. Wallace then began the discussion by asking some questions.

Mr. Wallace: 1. Is it not true that our Lord often set spiritual lessons before His disciples by material objects?

Dr. Stauffer: Let me say this, that in the form of your questions you are probably doing the same thing you did in regard to those household questions: you are asking your question in such a way that whatever answer I give, it will carry an implication.

Mr. Wallace: Doctor, why are you so afraid of those household questions?

Dr. Stauffer: You are making me say something in the form in which you ask the question that I didn't say, in order to get out the answer you want. I want you to be fair.

Mr. Wallace: It is not true? Don't you believe the Lord often set spiritual lessons before His disciples by material objects?

Dr. Stauffer: Yes, I do.

Mr. Wallace: 2. Is it not a common form of speech in any language to say, "this" for "this represents" or "signifies?"

Dr. Stauffer: No, I deny that.

Mr. Wallace: 3. Do you believe that when Christ took up bread, and broke it, it was His own body which He held in His hands, and which He Himself broke to pieces, and—

Dr. Stauffer: I believe just what Jesus said when He said, "Take eat, this is my body."

Mr. Wallace: Do you believe that it was His actual body He held in His hands?

Dr. Stauffer: His body was there—His body was present.

Mr. Wallace: You don't answer. Do you believe—

Dr. Stauffer: No, the bread wasn't His body.

Mr. Wallace: He didn't hold the body in His hands?

Dr. Stauffer: The bread wasn't His body, but He said, "This is my body, and my blood."

Mr. Wallace: Do you believe He held in His hands His body?

Dr. Stauffer: I don't know what He held. I know His hands were there —His body was there.

Mr. Wallace: 4. Do you believe Christ held His own blood in His hands?

Dr. Stauffer: That is a foolish question to ask.

Mr. Wallace: Answer it.

Dr. Stauffer: Certainly he didn't.

Mr. Wallace: 5. Had the body of Christ been broken and the blood shed when the Supper was instituted?

Dr. Stauffer: Blood shed? Yes.

Mr. Wallace: 6. Did not Jesus say, "This is my blood which is shed?"

Dr. Stauffer: Yes.

Mr. Wallace: Do you believe the blood had already been shed? Or, is that figurative language?

Dr. Stauffer: I don't think that this figurative. He said, "This is my body... This is my blood."

Mr. Wallace: "Which is shed." Do you believe the blood had already been shed, or is that a figurative expression?

Dr. Stauffer: "This is my blood of the covenant which is poured out for many unto the remission of sins"—that is what He said.

Mr. Wallace: Had it already been shed?

Dr. Stauffer: That is what He said.

Mr. Wallace: You believe Christ had already shed His blood?

Dr. Stauffer: He had shed some blood in Gethsemane, yes.[1]

Mr. Wallace: 7. Do you take the words, "This is my body...This is my blood," in a figurative or in a literal sense?

Dr. Stauffer: I take it for just what Jesus said: "This is my body."

Mr. Wallace: 8. What is the true body and true blood of Christ?

Dr. Stauffer: Why, the blood of Christ and the body. Anything else couldn't be the body and blood.

Mr. Wallace: You mean the true body is flesh?

Dr. Stauffer: The true body is human as well as divine.

Mr. Wallace: The true body of Christ is flesh?

Dr. Stauffer: I said it is His human body and divine being. The unity of Christ, the unity of His being, which is human and divine.

Mr. Wallace: When Christ said, "This is my body," He didn't mean this is my flesh?

Dr. Stauffer: I think He meant it is the flesh in the sense as we know it.

Mr. Wallace: 9. Doctor, where is the passage that says Christ gives "In, with, and under the bread, His true body?"

Dr. Stauffer: That isn't in the Bible.

Mr. Wallace: That is not in there?

---

[1] Editor's Note: Jesus had not yet gone to Gethsemane when He said, "This is my blood, which is shed..." It was after the Last Supper that Jesus went into Gethsemane to pray. See Matthew 26:26-36.

Dr. Stauffer: No.

Mr. Wallace: 10. Where is the scripture that teaches Christ gives in, with, and under the wine, His true blood?[2]

Dr. Stauffer: That expression isn't used. You see, that is what I am objecting to— the way in which you ask those questions.

Mr. Wallace: Where is the scripture that teaches in, with, and under the wine He gives His true blood?

Dr. Stauffer: He said, "Take eat, this is my body."

Mr. Wallace: That is the one you rely upon?

Dr. Stauffer: I take the word of Jesus.

Mr. Wallace: Do you not teach that in, with, and under the wine He gives us His true blood?

Dr. Stauffer: We teach that in the communion we receive the true body and blood of Christ.

Mr. Wallace: Upon what verse do you rely?

Dr. Stauffer: "Take, eat, this is my body."

Mr. Wallace: 11. Do not the Catholics teach that in the Lord's Supper they eat the body and drink the blood of the Lord?

Dr. Stauffer: Yes, they do.

Mr. Wallace: What is the difference in your teaching?

---

[2] The purpose for this question is explained in the final section of the book. It is a quote from the Lutheran Catechism.

Dr. Stauffer: They teach the bread and wine *actually* change into flesh and blood, and we don't *tell* how it is done; we simply take Jesus at His word. "Take eat, this is my body."

Mr. Wallace: 12. Can natural flesh be taken in a supernatural way?

Dr. Stauffer: Anything natural cannot be taken in a supernatural way.

Mr. Wallace: 13. Please cite chapter and verse for the supernatural presence of the body and blood of the Lord, in the communion service.

Dr. Stauffer: Supernatural? Any way the Lord is present, is supernatural.

Mr. Wallace: I mean His body and His blood—their presence.

Dr. Stauffer: "Take eat, this is my body."

Mr. Wallace: 14. Do the Scriptures teach that eating and drinking of the bread and wine give forgiveness of sins, life, and salvation?

Dr. Stauffer: We are promised forgiveness of sins because it is His sacrifice, and in the holy sacrament Christ is the same. He said take this bread and wine. This is the promise—my promise to you that in my death and through my death you are assured of the forgiveness of sins. I take that by faith in Christ. What He said is true, and He will remember that which is true. The promise is His promise and in the keeping of that and not apart from it.

Mr. Wallace: 15. Do you believe in taking Matthew 26:26 just as it is?

Dr. Stauffer: I take it for just what it says.

Mr. Wallace: Does not this text say "given" and "shed" for the remission of sins, and not "eaten" and "drunk" for the remission of sins?

Dr. Stauffer: Now, you see, there is another one of those forms of question. Jesus said, "Take eat, this is my body."

Mr. Wallace: I simply asked you what the text says. Does not the text say "given" and "shed" and not "eaten" and "drunk"?

Dr. Stauffer: Just wait, now; I will read Matthew 26:26 'And as they were eating, Jesus took bread and blessed it and brake it, and gave it to the disciples, and said, 'Take, eat, this is my body.' And He took the cup and gave thanks and gave it to them, saying, 'Drink ye all of it; for this is my blood of the new testament which is shed for many for the remission of sins.' "

Mr. Wallace: It was "given" and "shed"?

Dr. Stauffer: Yes.

Mr. Wallace: 16. Is it not possible to believe that the body was "broken" and the blood "shed" for the remission of sins and at the same time not believe that the actual "body" and "blood" of the Lord is present in the communion?

Mrs. Maack: We believe it is the real presence: the body and blood is present.

Dr. Stauffer: Is it possible to believe the body was broken and the blood shed for the remission of sins and not believe that the actual body and blood of the Lord is present in the communion? No; the actual body and blood of Christ is present in the communion, or it isn't a communion.

Mr. Wallace: 17. What right have you to deny the Lord's Supper to a Christian?

Dr. Stauffer: Paul said, "discerning the body and blood of Christ." If I give the communion to somebody I know is an open sinner and commits all kinds of sin, I am helping him.

Mr. Wallace: I said a "Christian," Doctor.

Dr. Stauffer: I am not here to define a Christian. How am I to judge?

Mr. Wallace: How are you to judge?

Dr. Stauffer: I don't.

Mr. Wallace: 18. Does not Jesus authorize the Lord's Supper as a memorial?

Dr. Stauffer: Yes, He says in Luke 22:19-20: "And He took bread and gave thanks and brake It, and gave unto them saying, 'This is my body which is given for you; this do in remembrance of me.' "

Mr. Wallace:

I. The Lord often set spiritual lessons before His disciples by using material objects.

I maintain, then, that in the text under discussion the Lord set a spiritual lesson before His disciples by using a material object. This was often His practice as is admitted by our friend, Dr. Stauffer. To show the truth of this premise, I am going to rely upon the text—upon the Bible.

First, let us notice the parable of the sower. In the parable, the sower is not used in a literal sense. A servant of God does not sow the seed of the Kingdom as a man might sow wheat seed. He does not sow literal seed. The seed is the Word of God. This can be seen to be a figurative expression because birds carried away the seed, and birds cannot carry away the Word of God. The Lord often used parables and this is plainly a parable.

In the fifteenth chapter of John, verse one, the Lord said, "I am the true vine and my Father is the husbandman." You will please notice that Jesus said, "I am the TRUE VINE." He did not say I represent a vine. He said I am the vine. Did Jesus mean to say that He was a grape vine?

Jesus also says, "I am the door," (John 10:7). Did He mean to say that He was a door like one that swings on hinges? He says I am the door. Is that literal or figurative? No one would be so foolish as to say that Jesus is a literal door, yet He himself says "I am the door." He did not say I represent a door, but I am the door.

In the tenth chapter of John, He also says, "My sheep hear my voice." Are the disciples of Jesus literal sheep? He calls them sheep. Does He teach that we are literal sheep? Mark you, that is what the text says: "My sheep."

Again, in John 1:36, John said, "Behold, the Lamb of God." Is Jesus an actual lamb? John plainly says that Jesus Christ is a lamb.

In Exodus 12:6-12, we find the record of the institution of the Passover. The Passover the children of Israel kept while in the Land of Palestine, and the Passover that Jesus and His disciples ate "represented" the actual Passover that was eaten in Egypt. The Passover that Jesus ate was a memorial of the one held in Egypt.

The "Passover" was a supper, yet the lamb was put for the Passover (Mk. 14:12). The lamb slain is called the Passover. This expression is used in connection with the Passover supper Jesus ate and in connection with the language the Doctor insists that should be taken literally. "And the first day of unleavened bread, when they kill the Passover." They killed the lamb which is here put for the Passover.

Jesus is called a rock. (I Cor. 10:4). Jesus is not a literal rock.

It can be just as easily proved that Jesus is a literal "lamb," "door," "vine," or a "rock" as to prove that "bread and wine" have with and under them the "true body and the true blood" of the Lord.

Jesus, knowing that even though we have spirits, we have bodies also, often addressed us through that medium. Thus He spoke in Matthew 26:26: "This is my body." It simply means this represents my body. "This is my blood" means this represents my blood. This could not do violence to the text as we have seen that Jesus often used forms of speech. This is bound to be true for the blood had not been shed. Jesus shed His blood in His death (John 19:34). Yet the text says, "For this is my blood... which is shed." (Matt. 26:28.) This must be a figure of speech for the blood had not been shed. It has to be a figure of speech as it was not a fact. A fact is something that has happened. The blood had not been shed, therefore, it could not be the "true" blood of Christ.

Dr. Stauffer: (interrupting) How is that?

Mr. Wallace: "This is my body" simply means this represents His body; "this is my blood," represents His blood.

Dr. Stauffer: I thought you took the Bible for what it says.

Mr. Wallace: I do.

Dr. Stauffer: He didn't say, "This represents my body." He said, "I am the vine:" of course, that is plainly figurative.

Mr. Wallace: Where does He say it is figurative?

Dr. Stauffer: Why, you can tell the way He uses it.

Mr. Wallace: I am going to show that you take part of Matthew 26:26-28 figuratively.

Dr. Stauffer: Go right ahead.

Mr. Wallace: Jesus says, "This is my blood" and He meant this represents His blood. This is bound to be true for the blood had not been shed. It has to be a figure of speech, as it was not a fact. A fact is something that has happened—something that has taken place. Jesus said, "This is my blood...WHICH IS SHED."

The Doctor is so anxious to make the expression, "This is my body" literal that he denies the atonement. He says that the blood of Christ had already been shed, that "Jesus shed some blood in Gethsemane." If the blood of Christ had already been shed, then Jesus died in vain. Why did Jesus die, if the blood had already been shed? In his zeal for this false doctrine, he denies the purpose of the cross of Christ.

He does not take the text "just as it is" because the "text as it is" does not teach what he teaches. He says that Jesus gave to the disciples His own flesh and blood to eat and drink, yet, in answer to the third question I asked him, he denies that Christ had His body in His hands. That which Jesus held in His hands is that which He called His body. The Doctor says that was not His own body which He held in His hands, and of which He and His disciples ate. I asked, "Do you believe that Jesus held His own blood in His hands?" He replied, "Certainly He did not." Then do you not take the text "just as it is" for the text "just as it is" says of the cup, "This is my blood."

Furthermore, he does not take the text for "just what it says" as the Doctor says things the text does not say. I asked, "Do the Scriptures teach that 'eating' and 'drinking' of the bread and wine give forgiveness of sins." He replied, "They do." However, the text does not say the bread and wine are "eaten" and "drunk" for the remission of sins, but "given" and "shed" for the remission of sins. You do not take the text, Matthew 26, "just as it is" because "just as it is" it does not teach that which you read into it.

The text says that the blood was already shed. "WHICH IS SHED." Knowing, then, that the blood had not been shed, we know that the language of Matthew 26:26-28 is figurative.

Dr. Stauffer: (interrupting) I said, "He shed some blood in the Garden of Gethsemane."

Mr. Wallace: Was the blood already shed?

Mrs. Maack: His blood was in the cup. He said so.

Dr. Stauffer: He hadn't died yet.

Mr. Wallace: He shed His blood in His death (John 19:34).

Dr. Stauffer: Yes, in His death.

Mrs. Maack: You are trying to pin something on us to justify yourself, which you can't do.

Mr. Wallace: No, the Doctor affirms that where it says, "I am the vine" is figurative language; then, he says that Matt. 26:26-28 must be taken literally. Yet, he won't take it literally. He says the blood was shed in the Garden, and now he says it was shed in His death. Such is the confusion of those who teach false doctrine. Now, when he says that Jesus shed His blood in His death—that the blood of Christ was not yet shed—in this way he says that the phrase, "which is shed," is bound to be a figure of speech. A figure of that which is to take place.

Dr. Stauffer: (interrupting) No, I didn't say that is bound to be a figure. Now, you make me say something I didn't say. I mean to take it for just what it says: that it is His body, and that it is His blood.

Mr. Wallace: Do you believe the blood had been shed?

Dr. Stauffer: I couldn't say a thing about that; I take the Scriptures just as they are. He was right with them, present in His human and divine form, which is Christ.

Mr. Wallace: The text SAYS the blood is shed—"Which IS shed."

Dr. Stauffer: What does that mean?

Mr. Wallace: It represents the blood that was to be shed.

Dr. Stauffer: How could He say, "is shed" if the blood was not shed; and yet He says, "is shed."

Mr. Wallace: My premise is, as I stated a moment ago, that the Lord often used figurative language. This is spoken of that which is signified or which is to come.

This truth can be further established by viewing our next premise:

II. It is a common form of speech in any language to say THIS IS, for THIS SIGNIFIES or THIS REPRESENTS.

This form of speech is very common in the English language. We would say (pointing to a picture of Martin Luther which hung on the wall), "This is Martin Luther." "This is Mrs. Stauffer," (referring to a picture of Mrs. Stauffer, the wife of the Doctor). Thus we see that in the English language, the phrase, "this is" is used to represent or signify.

Notice this manner of speech in the Bible. In Matthew the 13th chapter, Jesus gives us the parable of the sower. The "wayside" spoken of in verse four is referred to as "This is he." The "stony place" is called "he" in verse twenty.

"The same is he." Jesus speaks of the good ground as "he." "This is he that heareth the word. "This IS he," Jesus says. Thus, in the explanation of the parable, we see that Jesus uses the expression, "This IS" to represent or signify. "This IS he." The same IS he, "THIS IS he," is the way our Lord spoke in explaining the parable. Now, this reference proves it is a common form of speech to say, "This is" for "this represents" or "signifies."

In Genesis 41:26-27, we find the same use made of the phrase "This is." The seven good kine are seven years; and the seven good ears are seven years: the dream is one. "And the seven lean and ill-favored kine that came up after them are seven years..." Seven good kine are seven years. Seven ears are seven years. "Are" is the plural form of "is." Then, if seven kine are seven years, one kine would be one year. It would be right, then, to refer to the seven kine after this fashion, "These seven kine are seven years," and to one kine as, "This is one year."

So we see that in both the Old and New Testaments the expression "this is" is used to "represent or signify." Thus it is used in Matt. 26:26-28, This has been abundantly proved by showing the use of it in the Old and New Testaments and also by showing that the context will not allow a literal interpretation of it. To put a literal interpretation on it is to deny the atonement.

We do not eat the actual body and drink the actual blood of the Lord in the communion service. This truth can be further seen by viewing my next argument.

III. In the Lord's Supper, the Bible specifically says we eat the BREAD and drink the CUP.

Jesus took bread and said, "Eat." He told them to eat bread. He took the cup and said, "Drink" it. Thus we see that they were told to eat bread and drink the fruit of the vine. Three times, Paul says we eat "bread" and three times he says we drink the "cup." Not once did Jesus or Paul say that "In, with, and under the cup is the blood of the Lord." In fact, the Doctor says "There is no scripture that teaches that in, with, and under the bread is the true body of the Lord." What we eat in the Lord's Supper is bread and that which we drink is the cup—the fruit of the vine. Here is the matter as it now stands:

1. The Catholics say that they eat flesh— bread changed to flesh.

2. The Lutherans say "The body and blood of Christ is with, in, and under the bread and wine." (The Catholics eat the body straight, and

the Lutherans make a sandwich of it—they put it under the bread.)

3. Christians say "We eat the bread and drink the cup." That is what the Book tells us to do.

He affirms the body is supernaturally present. I asked: "Can natural flesh be taken in a supernatural way?" He says no. So, if you cannot eat natural flesh in a supernatural way (and thus you say you eat it) it must be changed, and so I find you teaching the doctrine of transubstantiation, the same as the Catholics.

Dr. Stauffer: (interrupting) No, we don't teach transubstantiation.

Mr. Wallace: I do understand, however, that you do eat the actual flesh of the Lord?

Dr. Stauffer: We eat the crucified body of Christ. He said, "Take, eat; this is my body...This is my blood."

Mr. Wallace: The Catholics say the bread is changed into the body of the Lord and the wine is turned into His blood. The only difference between the Lutheran and the Catholic is that they eat it straight and the Lutherans make a sandwich of it.

Dr. Stauffer: I say that when we take the sacrament connected with God's word and promise, He gives His entirety—His body and divinity. We partake of His being for He said, "My body is flesh indeed, and my blood is drink indeed."

Mr. Wallace: You eat the flesh of the Lord?

Dr. Stauffer: Sacramentally, yes, sir.

Mr. Wallace: If it is eaten sacramentally, it is changed, for you said natural flesh could not be taken in a supernatural way. If you eat the natural flesh of Christ, you do not eat it sacramentally. If you eat it sacramentally, you do not eat the natural flesh, as you affirm.

Dr. Stauffer: I said sacramentally because He was crucified.

Mr. Wallace: You affirm the Lord said, "This is my body" and now you say it is sacramentally His body,

Dr. Stauffer: What is the difference if it is Christ's body?

Mr. Wallace: The only difference is: the Catholics take it straight and you put it under the bread. You say it is actually present.

Dr. Stauffer: Yes, sir.

Mr. Wallace: Then you have a sandwich. You put the actual flesh of Christ in bread and eat it.

Dr. Stauffer: That is a little crude of you to say that, as holy a thing as that is. Christ said, "Take, eat; this is my blood and this is my body." It is not for me to say how. He said I will give you myself in the communion, and the Lutheran Church does not say how He does it. We only know that Christ said we receive His body and His blood as the food of our spirits; we receive it only as the crucified body, because He is crucified.

Mr. Wallace: We don't eat the actual body and blood of our Lord.

Dr. Stauffer: We do.

Mr. Wallace: We don't eat any flesh and drink any blood.

Dr. Stauffer: We do; we do not believe that it just represents.

Mr. Wallace: In answer to Question 1, the Doctor says he teaches that in, with, and under the bread is the true body of the Lord. Now, he says he doesn't say how. No wonder he is so afraid of my questions.

Having seen what the Lord's Supper is, we now call your attention to its purpose:

1, It is not to procure forgiveness of sins. Jesus did not say "eaten" and "drunk" for the remission of sins; He said "broken" and "shed." This body was "broken" and the blood was "shed" for the remission of sins. We do not "eat" and "drink" for the remission of sins. The Doctor will have to find a text that says "eaten" and "drunk" for the remission of sins. He goes to the text that says, "given" and "shed" for the remission of sins to prove his doctrine. Yet, he says this text must be taken "just as it is." Well, just as it is, it does not say that which you read into it. Why read into the text something that is not there?

2. The Lord's Supper is not a cannibalistic service where we either take the body of Christ straight or make a sandwich of it. To teach that you eat the actual, natural flesh and blood of Christ is to maintain a cannibalistic service. How can one claim to take Matthew 26 literally and then turn around and put a figurative meaning into it? It does not say in, with, and under the bread is the true body of the Lord. Yet, that is the text quoted to prove it. We do not eat flesh and drink blood. We do not engage in a cannibalistic service.

Dr. Stauffer: Neither do we take a cannibalistic service.

Mr. Wallace: You say you eat flesh.

Dr. Stauffer: We do—the crucified body and blood of Christ. It is the flesh of Jesus, His body. It is Christ; that is what we maintain: we are to partake of Christ in His human and divine unity. You can't divide His Humanity from His deity and yet claim it is Christ. The moment you divorce the human from the divine, you haven't the Christ. You only have part of Him. Jesus Christ, the Savior, was both man and God.

Mr. Wallace: He is afraid of these questions. If you eat the body of the Lord, you eat actual flesh. This cannot be done in a supernatural way—a spiritual way. Jesus says: "A spirit hath not flesh and bones as you see me having." (Luke 24:39). You cannot eat flesh spiritually. If you eat flesh, it is flesh, natural flesh.

3. The Lord's Supper is a communion service (I Cor. 1:16). The bread, when blessed, does not become the true body and the true blood of the Lord to the one partaking, but it becomes to him a communion of the body and a communion of the blood of the Lord. We eat bread and drink the cup and thereby have communion with the body and the blood of the Lord. The bread and cup do not become the actual—or, it is not the actual body and blood of the Lord. To us, it is a communion of the body and the blood of the Lord. "The cup of blessing which we bless, is it not a communion of the blood of Christ? The bread which we break, is it not a communion of the body of Christ?" This does not mean we eat the body of Christ, as may be seen from the context. "Have not they that eat the sacrifice, communion with the altar?" (I Cor. 10:18). "I would not that ye have communion with demons." "Ye cannot partake of the table of the Lord and the table of demons." Just as those who ate the sacrifice had communion with the altar, we in eating the Lord's Supper have communion with Christ.

Those who had communion with the altar, did not eat the altar. When it says they partook of the table of the Lord, does it mean they ate a literal table? They ate the sacrifice and thus had communion with the altar. We eat the bread and drink the cup and thus have communion with Christ. It is to us a communion service, and not a service where we eat the actual flesh of Christ. To offer, or eat, a sacrifice to a demon is to have communion with a demon. Surely, no one would be so foolish as to argue that to eat a sacrifice to a demon, is to eat a demon.

To have communion with the body of Christ does not mean to eat it. It is a communion of the body—not an eating of the body. In Luke 6:11, it is said, "They...communed one with another what they might do to Jesus." Did they eat one another? They communed one with another. "And two of them were going that very day to a village...and they communed with each other..." (Luke 24:14). Did they eat each other?

In the Lord's Supper, the bread is a communion of the body of the Lord. It does not become, nor have under it the actual body of Christ. It is a communion of the body of Christ. The cup is a communion of the blood of Christ. It is not the blood of Christ, nor does it have with and under it the blood of Christ. It is a communion with the blood of Christ.

4. The Lord's Supper is a memorial service. Jesus said, "This do, in remembrance of me." Paul says, "This do, in remembrance of me."

5. It proclaims the Lord's death. "For, as often as ye eat this bread and drink this cup, ye proclaim the Lord's death till He come." (I Cor. 11:26). Paul says it proclaims the Lord's death.

6. It is a service of hope. It is to be done with the hope of the coming of the Lord. It proclaims the Lord's death till he comes.

The Lord's Supper is a communion of the body and of the blood of the Lord, and not an eating of the "body" and the "blood" of the Lord. It is a service where bread is eaten and the cup is drunk, in remembrance of Jesus Christ.

Dr. Stauffer: In the sixth chapter of John, Jesus, talking to His disciples, said: "Except a man eat my flesh and drink my blood, ye have no life in you." Is that figurative?

Mr. Wallace: Yes.

Dr. Stauffer: He is not the bread of life?

Mr. Wallace: Not literal bread.

Dr. Stauffer: The expression: "He is the bread of life"—is that figurative?

Mr. Wallace: Yes; that is figurative.

Dr. Stauffer: Jesus said, "If any man eat of this bread"—that is clearly not bread made of wheat. Yet, Christ clearly says: "I am the bread of life"; yes, and the bread which I will give you is my flesh. What did he mean? Is that figurative, too—that He would give His flesh for the life of the world? "They strove one with another, saying, 'How can this man give us Himself to eat?'" That is just what men are doing today. The Lutheran Church does not answer how, but we say that is what Christ said. They strove among themselves, saying, "How can this man give us His flesh?" How can Christ give us His flesh in the communion? Jesus said, "This is my body...and this is my blood." He says it is Himself—not figurative. That is not figurative. "For my flesh is meat, indeed, and my blood is drink, indeed. He that eateth my flesh and drinketh my blood abides in me and I in him." Does that refer to the communion, or not?

Mr. Wallace: No, sir.

Dr. Stauffer: Do you think He didn't have in mind that He was going to institute the Lord's Supper when He said those words?

Mr. Wallace: I do not. He has reference to His death on the cross. The Doctor has a strange method of Bible interpretation. He makes one part of the verse literal and one part figurative as it suits his purpose. In John 6:51, "I am the bread which came down out of heaven; and if any man eat of this bread he shall live forever; yea, and the bread which I shall give is my flesh, for the life of the world." The Doctor says the expression, "I am the bread," is figurative—it is not bread of wheat. Yet, in the same connection, he says the word "meat" is literal. If bread is figurative, then "meat" is figurative. If "meat" is to be taken literally, then, "bread" has to be taken literally. In this way, then, you have proved Christ to be a common loaf of bread. The terms "bread" and "meat" are both used figuratively.

Dr. Stauffer: He knew He was going to institute the Lord's Supper. Jesus knew from the beginning who was to betray Him. He knew

Judas was going to betray Him. You say the Lord's Supper was instituted as a memorial. Is that right?

Mr. Wallace: Yes, sir.

Dr. Stauffer: Now, then; if it was a memorial (and that is the important thing—the memorial), may I ask you this question: Why is it that Matthew in the 26th chapter and the 26th and 27th verses (if that is the important thing) did not keep this in mind. If the memorial is the important thing, then tell me why Matthew didn't say something about the memorial in those verses. He doesn't refer to the memorial. Why did he leave it out?

Mr. Wallace: Doctor, the Lord's Supper was only instituted one time. These three records are of the same event—not three different events. The three writers that refer to the giving of the Lord's Supper all wrote about the same event. Now, since there was just one occasion on which the Supper was instituted, and one or more of the writers says that it was given as a memorial, it was said, was it not? Did all three of them have to say it, to make it so? A thing does not have to be repeated by God to make it true. Just once did the Lord institute the Supper, and on that one occasion He SAYS, "This do in remembrance of me."

Dr. Stauffer: Now, let us turn to Mark 14:22 and read there. "And as they did eat, Jesus took bread, and blessed, and brake it, and gave to them, and said, 'Take eat: this is my body. And He took the cup, and when He had given thanks, He gave it to them; and they all drank of it." Is there anything said there about a remembrance? If remembrance is the thing for which He instituted this service—and the important thing— why did Matthew and Mark omit it? If it wasn't the fact He was giving the body in the communion, why did He leave out remembrance—if that is the important thing? Luke mentions it. He said, "Do this in remembrance of me." So does Paul in L Cor. 10:16. You will acknowledge there are two of the gospels that don't mention remembrance at all, and you claim that is the important thing. When you come to Luke, he puts that in.

In the 10th chapter of Corinthians, Paul said: "The cup of blessing which we bless: is it not the communion of the blood of Christ? The bread which we break: is it not the communion of the body of Christ?" Not with the body, but of the body. Is it not a fact that when you receive the bread and wine, you receive the body and blood of Christ, in that you get what it stands for? In name, it is the body and blood of Christ, insofar as bread, He has said, is His body. He says over here farther, in the 11th chapter and 27th verse of I Corinthians, "Wherefore, whosoever shall eat this bread and drink this cup of the Lord unworthily, shall be guilty of the body and blood of the Lord." Now, if the body and blood of Christ are not present in the communion, how could he be guilty of the body and blood of Christ—that which is not present, only a memorial? Paul says: "For as often as ye eat this bread and drink this cup, ye do shew the Lord's death till He comes." "For he that eateth and drinketh unworthily, eateth and drinketh damnation to himself." Paul says, "Do this in remembrance of me."

Let me illustrate: I send that young lady a box with a beautiful necklace in it, and I say to her, "When you receive this, do receive it in remembrance of me." Has she received the jewels? She has. But I say, "You take this, you receive it, but, when you do receive it, receive it in remembrance of me." She has it. The fact that she does it in remembrance of me doesn't mean she hasn't received the jewels. And when I take Christ in communion and remembrance, it can't mean I haven't received Christ.

Mr. Wallace: (interrupting) Your illustration of the necklace amuses me. You sent the young lady a box containing a necklace and say, "When you receive this, do receive it in remembrance of me. Has she received the jewels?" According to your teaching on the Lord's Supper (the thing you strive to illustrate), when she opened the box she would not find the necklace but she would find you. You argue that when Christ took bread and said, "Eat this in my memory," that instead of its being just that very thing, you find Christ Himself in the bread. So, I guess the young lady would find you in the box, and not the necklace—or, therein find both you and the necklace.

Dr. Stauffer: I maintain that when Jesus spoke those words in the 6th Chapter of John, He knew He was going to institute the Lord's Supper, and Matthew and Mark neither one refer to remembrance. If that is the important thing, tell me why they left it out and refer only to "This is my body." Paul says, if you don't discern the body of Christ, you eat and drink condemnation unto your soul. He says: This is my body, and He says you receive my body and blood—it is food to your souls. "I am the bread of Life." He is the bread of life—the one upon which we stand.

We maintain that the Bible is God's word and contains His promise, and in baptism we receive what He has promised: the forgiveness of sins, eternal life, deliverance from death and the devil, as His word and promises declare. We believe that in the communion, we receive what He says: His body and His blood—for the fruits of that new life that has been begotten within us through the rite of baptism that He has promised. Then, this new life which is begotten by the Holy Spirit through the rite of baptism that He has promised. Then this now which is begotten by the Holy Spirit through the Word and promise in baptism, that we have received what He promised, not because you or I have been baptized, but because that is what Jesus said; and we cling to what Jesus said. We maintain that God has given through Christ salvation, and in baptism He bestows the Holy Spirit. The Holy Ghost is the regenerating power, and the new life is begotten in you by the Holy Ghost—not by water.

If I receive Christ, I must receive Christ in His human and divine nature, because if you separate the human nature from Christ you haven't Christ, and if you separate the divine nature from the humanity of Christ, again you haven't Christ. Christ was man and God, and we receive this total man in the communion as the food for our spirit life. We believe in the communion, we do confess Christ, and we confess to all the world that we receive Christ as our Savior. We commemorate Christ's death in that communion, and I take Him in the communion, receiving Him in the communion for the assurance of the forgiveness of sins and for the strengthening of my spirit life, for He is the bread of life.

There is no signifying—He does not say "signify." I will grant you that there are in the Bible many things that are plainly to be interpreted in a figurative sense, and by taking what goes before and what follows after, and what goes between, you may determine. When He says, "Take, eat; this is my body," and didn't refer to the memorial as the thing, and Paul says if you don't discern the body, the person receiving it only as a communion, does not receive the full significance of the communion which is the presence and the partaking of Jesus Christ for the food of our souls. When I receive that blood and wine, God imparts His very self to me and because of that I am strengthened—I am fed upon it. I leave it to anybody if that isn't a wonderful consolation to sinful man. I think it is one of the finest teachings of the whole Bible. If it had been intended for a memorial, then certainly Matthew wouldn't have omitted that, and the fact it is done for a memorial wouldn't exclude the body and blood of Christ.

I gave this young lady a jewel box with a beautiful jewel in it, and I said, "When you do receive it, I ask you to receive it as a memorial of me." But she has received it. When Jesus said, "Take, eat; this is my body" and gave Himself to me and said do this, He doesn't say He hasn't given Himself to me because I am to remember Him for this one sacrifice. We believe that the person who sees that in it, doesn't lose anything; but the person who can't see that teaching doesn't comprehend and discern the body of Christ, and loses to that extent the thing for which Jesus Christ really instituted the Holy Communion.

Am I bringing condemnation on myself for believing that as it reads there? Surely, I am not losing anything—I am gaining Him. But the person who doesn't see that and who doesn't see the body of Christ, I would say doesn't see all that is in the communion. That is one of the most sublime doctrines of the Bible, and our church stands for that. We believe that. We receive the Christ as He said. "I am the bread of life." "Here is my body"—and He gave it to me. Whether that bread is changed or not, we do say it is not.

So, you see, my brother, you and I aren't a thousand miles apart. We believe in God, the Father. We believe in Jesus Christ as the Savior. We believe in the Holy Spirit and His work in the hearts and lives of men, and those things are to show us that we are sinners and Christ is our Savior. We believe all that—so the facts of the matter are: we aren't a thousand miles apart.

(Close of Dr. Stauffer's Speech. Meeting Dismissed.)

FACTS CONCERNING THE PUBLICATION OF THIS DEBATE

A STATEMENT BY MR. WALLACE

Since Dr. Stauffer has made a statement concerning why he does not want the discussion between us published, I hereby make a statement as to why I took a stenographer with me to report the debate and why I desire it published.

1. All arrangements were made and perfected by Dr. Stauffer. He was moderator, time keeper, chairman, and speaker. Without a neutral man for moderator what guarantee did I have that I would even be heard?

2. He refused to sign a specific proposition. The following proposition was sent to him and he refused to sign it.

"The Scriptures authorize infant baptism."

_____________ Affirms

<u>G. K. Wallace</u> Denies

I was simply told that he wanted to talk about "infant baptism" and the "Lord's Supper." The Dr. knew what points he desired to discuss in particular and yet refused to divulge them to me. I went there not knowing what he intended to affirm about these subjects. Having refused to sign specific propositions and thus put me to such disadvantage I think the Doctor's complaint about unfairness comes with poor grace. The legs of the lame are not equal.

3. The discussion was not held on neutral ground, I was simply his guest and he being host, moderator, time keeper—in fact having assumed ALL AUTHORITY—I could have been asked to leave without even being heard.

4. The debate was held behind closed doors. I insisted on inviting the public and this he refused to do. Dr. Stauffer decided just who should come and who should not come, O, the fairness of Dr. Stauffer.

5. Being held behind closed doors, where the public could not hear, I was afraid of misrepresentations of what I would say. A closed discussion usually creates more talk than an open one. I anticipated this correctly. What I said has been greatly misrepresented and distorted.

6. I desired the young people for whose benefit the discussion was held have a copy so they can study it carefully at home, where there is not the excitement of an oral discussion.

The following is the letter sent to Dr. Stauffer from the printing company.

THE ZONA PRINTING COMPANY
416-18 N. Water St. Phone 4-3014
Wichita, Kansas June 17, 1937

Dear Dr. Stauffer:

Please call us when this manuscript is ready as we have the contract to print this book and are ready to work on it.

We have been requested to have you sign the attached statement.

ZONA PRINTING COMPANY
Wm. D. Anderson, Mgr.
Wichita, Kansas
June 17, 1937

Having carefully examined the Report of the within discussion, reported by Miss Norfleet, and compared it with our notes and memoranda, we believe it to be a full exhibition of the statements and arguments made by us in the conference we held Sunday afternoon, March 7. 1937, at Wichita, Kansas, and hereby certify that the readers have a fair representation of the discussion.

Signed <u>G. K. Wallace</u>

Signed ____________

In reply to the above request, Dr. Stauffer sent me the following statement—a carbon—copy—having sent the original to the printer.

A STATEMENT BY DR. STAUFFER

The latter part of May, Mrs. Inez Maack called me to her home at which time she said that her son, William and a Miss Herrington, were engaged to be married and that there was difference in their religious beliefs. She asked me if I would be willing to meet with her pastor, a Rev. Wallace, the girl's father, herself and myself to discuss these differences with them. I told her that I would not enter into any debate but that since she asked it, I would be willing to meet them in my study and tell them what we believed the Bible taught on the subjects under discussion, and agreed to an arrangement for such a meeting in my study March 7th, 1937.

A little later a request came that instead of her pastor his brother, a minister of that church should be permitted to do the speaking at the meeting. I was not entirely pleased at the change but agreed to it.

When the time for the meeting arrived the party met and Mr. Wallace brought with him a stenographer. That was a surprise to me but thinking he wanted a stenographic report that he might refer to what was said, I made no objections. The conversations were well-reported. Only a few mistakes.

But what was my great surprise to receive through the mail a copy of the conversations with a statement that Mr. Wallace expected to have the proceedings printed and a request that I look over the notes. This I did and made some corrections and observations. I felt that that was taking an undue advantage since nothing had been said about printing the conversations and what I had said in the conference was not with any idea that what was said was to be given to the public in printed form. Yet I did not say I objected, for I felt that while under the circumstances I preferred it should not be done, I realized Mr. Wallace had the material and probably would do with it as he liked.

Now I am asked to sign a document certifying to certain things regarding the materials which is practically giving my consent to its publication. This I do not wish to do for many reasons, principally these:

1. It was not my understanding when I consented to the conference that the talks were to be taken by a stenographer for publication,

2. Not having been given, on my part, with that intention, they are not in the form that I would wish them to be given in printed form to the public.

3. If I desired to give my personal beliefs and that of my Church to the public I would not prefer to do it in the manner proposed.

4. It was not my intention to give to Mr. Wallace material from which he would make capital.

5. There are statements made by Mr. Wallace to Mrs. Maack during the discussion that should not appear in a public document, since it will undoubtedly give a wrong impression.

6. That there are many books and pamphlets in print that set forth the teachings and doctrines of the Lutheran Church in much better form than in the document which Mr. Wallace proposes to have printed.

7. The printing of the proceedings of the conference is all together apart from the purpose of the conference. For these reasons as well as others not stated I cannot give my consent to the proposed publication.

E.E. STAUFFER.

REPLY TO DR. STAUFFER

1. *"It was not my understanding when I consented to the conference that the talks were to be taken down by a stenographer for publication."*

I was asked to meet Dr. Stauffer and yet given no assurance as to the NATURE of the debate. However, he knew before he spoke even one word that it was being taken down. To this he did not object. Regardless of his understanding at the time he "consented to the conference" he knew it was being taken down while he spoke. I introduced the stenographer to him and told him that she came for the purpose of taking it down. He made no objection.

2. *"Not having been given, on my part, with that intention, they are not in the form I would wish them to be given in printed form to the public."*

He should not have made his speeches if he did not want them taken down. He knew what was going on. The following letters shows that I did not take advantage of Mr. Stauffer. This letter written April 12, 1937.

Dear Dr. Stauffer:

I am mailing you under separate cover the transcript of your statements made in the little discussion we had. For the sake of some who were not permitted to attend and to clarify statements about what was said, I desire to publish the transcript so my people may know the facts.

Please feel free to make the necessary corrections in your speeches. You know what you believe and perhaps, you know better than anyone else what you said. So far as I am concerned you may clarify and strengthen the arguments you made, however, do not add new material, that is, new arguments.

Mr. Stauffer read and corrected his speeches and made some notes on mine. At the same time he said it was all right to go ahead and publish them. He kept the transcript for over one month. He read and corrected it and told me personally that it was all right to publish it. I think his objections come with poor merit at this late hour. Had I been trying to take the advantage of him WHY DID I EVER LET HIM HAVE THE TRANSCRIPT? The fact that he had possession of the transcript for such a long period of time and was at liberty to do with it as he pleased shows beyond a doubt that I was not unfair in the matter,

3. *"If I desired to give my personal beliefs and that of my church to the public I would not prefer to do it in the manner proposed."*

This is a true statement. He had rather someone would not expose the sophistry of his arguments. Lutheran doctrine, like Catholicism thrives better in the dark. Neither will stand investigation.

4 *"It was not my intention to give to Mr. Wallace material from which he would make capital."*

"Capital" is defined by Webster, (one meaning), as "anything that serves to increase one's power or influence." So, dear reader, I was not thus trying to do. However, I did take a stenographer with me to report the debate so you would know just what happened. In this way I did forestall the Dr.'s effort to make "capital" of a situation over which he had complete control. The stories that have been told as to what was said have been varied. By reading the book you will know the truth.

5. *"There are statements made by Mr. Wallace to Mrs. Maack during the discussion that should not appear in a public document, since it would undoubtedly give the wrong impression."*

This is the more reason that I want it published. The Dr. is making "capital" of what I said to Mrs. Maack. This discussion, controlled by him is being used as a wedge to counteract the defeat his doctrine suffered at the hands of truth. As long as he can make people believe that I said things to a woman that should not appear in a public document he can prejudice them against me and the truth of God as I presented it. I am willing for the public to know what I said to Mrs. Maack. More than that, I am ANXIOUS for them to know what I said. I was asked to meet Dr. Stauffer but I found out that I had to deal with him and Mrs. Maack. Why did she enter into this any way? Mrs. Maack, no doubt was much displeased with the efforts of her pastor. She felt sure that he could prove that babies should be baptized and when Dr. Stauffer failed to do so she could not hold her peace. However, dear reader, Dr. Stauffer did as well as any man can do in defending his doctrine. The weakness was not in the man but in the doctrine. No man can do better than he did and few will try. I hereby challenge any man in the Lutheran church, from the President on down, to debate the issue with me. Let us have a discussion of several days duration with rules, moderators and specific propositions and then we will not be disturbed by a third party. Before, I was challenged and now I offer the challenge.

6. *"That there are many books and pamphlets in print that set forth the teaching and doctrine of the Lutheran Church in much better form than in the document which Mr. Wallace proposes to have printed."*

This statement is true. The book in your hands does not set forth the Lutheran doctrine as he would like it. In fact it exposes the Lutheran doctrine—It shows wherein it is wrong. That is the reason he does not want you to read it. He had much rather you would read some of their literature where no one has a chance to reply. In replying to a letter to Mrs. Maack I wrote:

> In your closing remarks, you requested that I secure Dr. Martin Luther's Small Catechism. I have one of these Catechisms and had carefully and thoroughly read it before I met Dr. Stauffer. You remember that he was so afraid of my

questions. Also, you remember how he complained about them, the unfairness of them, how I was trying to trap him, to lead him into something he did not believe, and yet these questions were based upon the teachings of this Catechism. For instance, on page 142 of said Catechism, I read, "In, with and under the bread, He gives us His true body; in, with and under the wine, He gives us His true blood." Now, the only difference in this statement and my questions to Dr. Stauffer is this: I took the affirmative statements in the Catechism and simply made questions of them. For instance, in regard to this I said, "Dr. Stauffer, do you believe that in, with, and under the bread He gives His true body?" I also framed a question of the same nature in regard to the wine, so you see I was perfectly familiar with the Catechism, in fact, I knew too much about it to suit Dr. Stauffer.

Now Mrs. Maack, let me give you a little kindly advice as you advised me what to read. Lay aside Luther's Catechism. There would be no Lutherans if they only knew the Bible. Just take your New Testament or the Bible, read it and obey it. Leave all the creeds and catechisms where they belong—and they belong in bon-fires and not in Christian homes. This is the reason that you are a Lutheran, because you have been studying the Catechism. The doctrines of Luther are not in the Bible, if so why the Catechism? If you say the doctrines in the Catechism were taken from the Bible, who authorized anybody to take them out? And if they were taken out of the Bible they ought to be put back where God put them and leave them where it pleased Him. You could not for the sake of your life get an idea that babies ought to be baptized by reading the Bible. To find this out you have got to turn to some creed or Catechism, therefore leave your creeds and Catechisms and follow only the Bible...I notice the Catechism says, "God's Word and Luther's doctrines shall to eternity endure." You people do not even believe in Luther's doctrines because you wear his name in opposition to both Martin Luther and the Lord Jesus Christ. Martin Luther, according to Michelet, page 662, said, "I pray you, leave my name alone; and not call yourselves Lutherans but Christians. Who is Luther? My doctrine is not mine. I have not been crucified for any one. St. Paul, I Cor. 1:13, would not that any should call themselves of Paul nor of Peter, but of Christ. How, then does it befit me a miserable bag of dust and ashes, to give my name to the children of Christ? Cease, my dear friends, to cling to these party names and distinctions. Away with them all, and let us call ourselves Christians, after him from whom our doctrines comes."

So, the Dr. would much rather have you read some of their literature where you could not see their teaching compared with the Word of God. This is another reason I want the debate published. I want you to see the truth of God contrasted with the Doctrines of Martin Luther.

7. *"The printing of the proceedings of the conference is all together apart from the purpose of the conference."*

Who denies this? The purpose of the conference was to discuss our differences. The purpose of the printing of this is to let people see what we said while we discussed our differences. The printing of this is to correct false reports about what was said in the conference. The purpose is to show that not one thing I said to a woman should not go into a public document. The purpose is to let people know just what took place behind the closed doors and in the conference over which the Dr. had complete control. The purpose is to give the young people for whose benefit the debate was held a copy of the discussion so they may carefully read and study it. Why does the Dr. not want them to have a copy? If the Dr. is really interested in those young people knowing the truth why did he not help bear the expense of this so they would have a copy? I was so anxious for them to know the truth and carefully study our statements that I said to Dr. Stauffer under date of April 12, "All the expense involved in this transaction, I myself will bear." Instead of the Dr. trying to get the truth before them he is now trying to keep the truth away from them.

"For these reasons as well as others not stated I cannot give my consent to the proposed publication."

On June 18, 1937, he refused to sign a statement which reads as follows: "Having carefully examined the report of the within discussion, reported by Miss Norfleet, and compared it with our notes and memoranda, we believe it to be a full exhibition of the statements and arguments made by us in the conference we held Sunday afternoon, March 7th, 1937, at Wichita, Kansas, and hereby certify that the readers have a fair representation of the discussion."

Signed, <u>G. K. Wallace</u>

Signed, _____________

The Dr. is as careless in reading this statement as he is in reading his Bible. He tries to justify infant baptism by a passage that mentions neither infants nor baptism. Now he thinks the above statement is asking his permission to publish the debate. In this he is wrong. I had that permission already. In this he was asked to say that he had read the transcript, corrected it and believed it to be a fair report of the discussion. However, the statement he did sign is just as good as the one we asked him to sign. We asked that he state that he had examined he transcript and in the above statement of Dr. Stauffer please note these words:

"The conversations were well reported. Only a few mistakes....This I did and made some corrections and observations."

So, dear reader, the preceding pages, according to Dr. Stauffer, contains a correct report of the debate. He says only a few mistakes were made. The Dr. made corrections and observations and returned the transcript and in his own words, "Yet I did not say I objected." Up to this point the Dr. did not object to its being published. He told me in his study that he did not object to my publishing it.

When does the Dr. object?

1. He objects after he had read, corrected and returned the transcript with his permission to publish it.

2. He objects, after giving his permission to publish it and after that I had advertised it among my people.

3. He objects the day the contract is let to the printer.

The discussion was held March 7th and the contract for publication was let on June 17th. Over three months passed and the Dr. did not object. In fact during this time he read, corrected, and returned the transcript and orally gave me his permission to publish it. Yet his objection at this late hour was not accompanied by a check to defray at least a part of the expense to which I had been put by his own consent.

Under the date of June 18th Dr. Stauffer writes:

Rev. G. K. Wallace,
Wichita, Kansas.

Dear Mr. Wallace:

I am enclosing a copy of a statement which I am sending to the printer regarding the publication of the conversations in our conference held in March. I have no doubt that you will be disappointed but I cannot give my consent for the publication of the same and if you do publish them it must be upon your own responsibility.

Yours sincerely,

Dr. E. E. Stauffer.

I see no reason why I should not publish the debate.

He read and corrected the transcript and told me to go ahead and publish it. Why should he try to stop it now after I have gone to so much expense?

Doctor Stauffer has constantly complained about unfairness on my part. Remember these facts:

1. I was requested to meet him in discussion. He made all the arrangements.

2. The only requests I made were completely ignored. I asked for an open discussion in the regular way—with moderators, time keepers and specific propositions.

3. He had time to examine and correct the transcript before publication. This he did and said it was all right to publish it.

4. He knew that it was to be published while he had possession of it. Why did he not refuse to correct and return it if he did not desire it published? He was asked to read and correct it for publication and this he did. Having read and corrected it for that purpose—that is for the purpose of printing—it comes with poor favor to try to stop it on the day the contract is let for publication.

5. The Dr. says, "The conversations were well reported". Thus in his own words the book is a fair representation of the debate.

6. In conversation with him on the telephone I offered to give him five thousand words to try and patch up his efforts,

7. He claims he was not prepared to make a public statement. Is it true that a man who has preached for years and years, for fifteen years for one church cannot make a statement as to what he

believes? He made preparations for the debate. Too, he read most of his speech out of a book.

I am sorry that this personal element had to enter into this. Such would not have been the case, if Dr. Stauffer had allowed me to go ahead with the publication, according to our understanding, when the transcript was corrected and returned.